Quantum Miracles

Unlocking Hidden Laws That Govern Miracles

Steve McVey

TWS Publishing

TWS Publishing
Lodi, CA
www.thewriterssocietypublishing.com

Paperback ISBN 978-1-966818-01-4

Contents

CHAPTER 1

MIRACLES AREN'T MAGIC

For centuries, miracles have been regarded as divine interruptions, supernatural interventions that defy the known laws of nature and override the ordinary flow of cause and effect. Most religious traditions have taught us that miracles are rare, reserved for extraordinary circumstances, and cloaked in mystery, far beyond our comprehension. Meanwhile, skeptics have dismissed them outright, arguing that there's no room in science for the miraculous.

But what if both views are missing something fundamental? What if miracles aren't violations of natural law at all, but revelations of how reality actually works on a deeper level? St. Augustine is reputed to have said, "Miracles are not contrary to nature, but only contrary to what we know about nature."

C.S. Lewis pointed toward this in *The Lion, the Witch and the Wardrobe* when he distinguishes between the "deep magic" and a "deeper magic from before the dawn of time."[1] The first represents the laws known and accepted by the visible world. They're rules that even the White Witch claims authority over. But the deeper magic is what governs Reality beneath the surface. It's a higher law that transcends the limited understanding of those living only on the surface level of existence. When Aslan rises from the dead, it is not because he breaks the law, but because he acts in accordance with a deeper law that the Witch didn't know existed.

What if Augustine and Lewis were right? What if miracles aren't interruptions but invitations? A sort of unveiling of the hidden architecture of the cosmos, framed by a divine intelligence and waiting for our recognition and participation?

That question defines the reason I wrote this book. I want you to see that miracles are not anomalies or rare spiritual rewards. They are your birthright. They aren't magic tricks. They aren't doled out to a privileged spiritual elite. They're not conditional on how many hours you've prayed or how intensely you've worshiped. They aren't handed out like gold stars for good religious behavior.

Miracles emerge from immutable spiritual and scientific laws that govern the entire universe. And lest anybody assume that bringing science into this discussion diminishes the role of God, let me be clear: these laws don't avoid giving God credit where credit is due. To the contrary, they were established by God and are how He operates. When I smuggled Bibles into China, I flew on a plane governed by the law of aerodynamics. That law made my journey possible. Now, rewind history: ask somebody before the Wright brothers took flight in 1903 if air travel would require a miracle, and they wouldn't hesitate to say yes.

Back then, it was unthinkable. Today, we board planes without thinking twice about it. What changed? Our understanding of the laws at play. Could it be that other miracles we now consider impossible might become equally familiar as we awaken to more of the divine design? Could God have built other natural laws into the universe that are waiting to be discovered? Might there be laws that make the miraculous more accessible than we've imagined? Einstein said, "There are only two ways to live your life. One is as though nothing is a miracle. The other is as though everything is a miracle." What if we expanded our definition of miracles to include what we once thought impossible? What if we lived from the understanding that the miraculous isn't rare, but at the very core of our divine DNA?

Since the rise of quantum physics in the 20th century, we've reached a turning point. We no longer need to pit science against faith. The two are not enemies. In fact, they're becoming partners in unveiling the overwhelming beauty of how this universe actually works. Our growing grasp of quantum mechanics is beginning to show that many events previously labeled "miraculous" align surprisingly well with the nature of reality at its most fundamental level.

God is speaking through science. Don't shy away from that. The Bible says, "The heavens declare the glory of God," and astronomy echoes that. Isaiah said that "the trees of the field clap their hands" to celebrate God's goodness and along comes botany affirming the fact. Throughout this book, you'll see how science gives a decisive "Amen!" to many truths found in the Bible. It's time we move past the tired old narrative of Darwin vs. Jesus and embrace the thrilling truth that science is, in many ways, catching up to what faith has proclaimed all along.

THE CHANGING LANDSCAPE OF SCIENCE AND FAITH

For too long, science and faith have been treated like two opposing teams. The Enlightenment ushered in an age of empirical reasoning that explained everything through material causes, leaving little room for spiritual realities. In reaction, many religious circles dug in and retreated into blind faith. Science was viewed with suspicion.

That divide is quickly dissolving. A new paradigm is up-and-coming. Some of the most brilliant minds in science are now acknowledging that the purely materialistic worldview is insufficient. They are recognizing that there is more than has met the eye. Einstein once said, "The most beautiful thing we can experience is the mysterious. It is the source of all true art and all science."[2] And Max Planck, the father of quantum theory, went even further: "All matter originates and exists only by virtue of a force... I must assume behind this force the existence of a conscious and intelligent mind. This mind is the matrix of all matter."[3]

Science is beginning to echo what faith has always whispered: that the world isn't just physical material moving predictably. Reality is more like a field of infinite potential, shaped by unseen forces, consciousness, and observation.

A Personal Reflection: When Science Met My Faith

I remember when I first began to see the connection between science and faith. The deeper I delved into quantum mechanics, the more I realized that the fabric of the universe is far more mysterious than we were taught in school or church. I remember reading a physicist explain the concept of quantum superposition, that a single particle can exist in multiple places at once. Instantly, my mind went to the biblical truth where the Bible says we are seated with Christ in the heavenly place while simultaneously being here on planet Earth. So, science gave me a framework for better understanding what I'd only been able to take by faith.

Then, I came to study the quantum concept of entanglement, where two particles are of the same essence and are one, even though they may be in two different locations. The quantum truth teaches that one is not only connected to the other but is defined by it so that whatever is true of the other is equally valid of its counterpart. This facet of quantum mechanics reminded me of the Bible's teaching that we are one with Christ, and our lives are defined by Him. Christ is not simply in your life. He is your life. He defines you. So, again, science was helping me better understand my Bible. Who knew that electrons and epistles could end up in the same conversation?

As I studied, new discoveries came to me. My research into this modern science changed everything. It was as if the walls between science and spirituality crumbled before my eyes to reveal a single, coherent truth: Faith doesn't contradict science. At least not contemporary science. It completes it. Miracles are not violations of natural law; they are the fulfillment of it at its highest level.

The Quantum Connection to Miracles

Quantum physics has broken the old Newtonian mold of a rigid, mechanical universe. Superposition reveals a reality where particles can exist in multiple potential states at once (in heaven and on earth), where the observer affects the outcome (that's science preaching faith), and where particles can be instantaneously linked across great distances (union with Christ).[4] These discoveries unveil a universe that is so much more alive, interconnected, and responsive than we've ever imagined. When we understand that true science shows how the Creator works in His creation, we can see that Jesus wasn't denying science but displaying it at a higher level.

The shift toward a miraculous life starts inside. Not with bigger faith, but with deeper awareness. You don't need to try to get more faith like it's some kind of holy Bitcoin. You've already got it. Paul said, "The life I now live, I live by the faith of the Son of God." It's His faith you're depending on. The only thing left to do is elevate your mindset.

Jesus performed miracles that may be better understood today through a quantum lens. Things such as healing at a distance, walking on water, or feeding multitudes are quantum slam-dunks when we understand it. We'll explore the quantum principles behind these in Chapter 4.

If you haven't read my other books on quantum themes, some of the terms used here might sound unfamiliar at first. Don't worry—we'll explore them together in the chapters ahead. For now, just know this: The miracles recorded in Scripture are not one-time stunts meant to wow the crowds. They are windows into how reality functions when we operate from our true position, seated with Christ in the dimension of the Kingdom.

Expanding on Biblical Miracles: A Deeper Look

Take the story of the woman with the issue of blood. She touched the hem of Jesus' robe and was instantly healed. Jesus turned and said, "Your faith has made you well" (Mark

5:34). What happened there? It appears that her act of faith created an instance of quantum resonance that synched her internal frequency with the frequency of divine healing. In my book *Quantum Faith*, I talked about how particles vibrate at different frequencies, and how resonance can amplify quantum effects. Was Jesus revealing this scientific principle millennia before science caught up? It sure looks like it.

Or consider Lazarus. Jesus didn't just pray; He commanded: "Lazarus, come forth!" (John 11:43). Sound waves carry energy. They affect matter. It seems likely that Jesus' words held the exact energetic frequency needed to reboot Lazarus' body at the molecular level.

MIRACLES ARE NOT JUST FOR THE PAST

One of the greatest misconceptions in Christian thought is that miracles are locked in the past. Many believe them to be limited to Bible times but no longer accessible today. Some have been taught that miracles were signs meant only to establish Jesus' authority as if God has since withdrawn this reality from the world. Others believe miracles still happen but are unpredictable, occurring only if God intervenes for reasons beyond our understanding. But Jesus said something staggering: "Whoever believes in me will do the works I have been doing, and they will do even greater things than these" (John 14:12). If His miracles were one-time anomalies, why promise their continuation and expansion?

Miracles were never meant to be rare, random, or restricted. They are invitations into a way of living grounded in divine design. We don't need to beg for them. We need to understand them. Miracles follow the principles of the Kingdom, and once we align with those principles, we move into the flow of the miraculous.

An Invitation to Explore

It doesn't take a scientist to appreciate the connections between quantum physics and miracles. You don't have to trade in your childlike faith for a lab coat. In my book, *Quantum Life*, I wrote much about how "The kingdom of God is within you" (Luke 17:21). This suggests that the ability to engage with divine reality is already present within each of us. We only need to learn how to access it.

So, as you read this book, I invite you to approach it with curiosity. Be willing to openly reflect on new perspectives. Ask questions. Consider the possibility that what you might have thought was supernatural is part of the natural order; a part we are only beginning to understand.

Miracles are not magic. They aren't reserved for a spiritually exclusive minority. They are the natural overflow of a far more wonderful reality than we've been taught to believe. As you continue this journey, you may find that the miraculous isn't as distant as it once seemed. It is, and always has been, within reach.

Chapter 2

Miracles Should Be Normal

For many, miracles seem like anomalies, exceptional moments that defy the laws of nature, often consigned to religious writings or personal testimonies and far removed from everyday experience. They are often viewed as unpredictable, uncommon occurrences that only happen to a select few, people blessed with extraordinary faith or chosen for some divine purpose most of us won't ever experience. I've already suggested that this viewpoint is fundamentally flawed. But let me repeat something I said in Chapter 1, because this seed needs watering: What if miracles weren't supposed to be rare? What if they're not the exception but the rule? What if they are meant to be an integral part of the human experience, divinely woven into the very fabric of existence, waiting for us to recognize their presence and engage with them? Will you begin to shift your mind in that direction? The question isn't just rhetorical. It can lead to a new life. Think about the possibilities!

The idea that miracles should be a regular part of life isn't new. Jesus and his disciples lived with an expectation of the supernatural. They were confident that divine power was readily available to manifest the kingdom of God on earth in amazing ways. Their lives demonstrated this unwavering belief as evidenced by countless supernatural occurrences. The Bible is filled with accounts of miracles. These stories are testaments to the power of faith and the willingness of God to consistently act in our lives. Yet, over time, much of Western society and even the church lost its expectation of miracles as a part of daily life. Culture surrendered to a more rationalistic and materialistic worldview. We stopped expecting miracles because we have been conditioned to think that the supernatural is separate from the natural. We've often seen it as existing in a realm outside our everyday experience. We have lost sight of the fact that, in Reality, they are the same. The supernatural and natural are interwoven aspects of a single, unified reality called "the field" or "the matrix" by scientists and "the kingdom of God" by the Bible.

MIRACLES AND THE NATURE OF REALITY

The world we perceive with our five senses is only a fraction of what exists. It is a limited perspective that hides the vastness of the underlying Reality. The human eye can see only about 0.0035% of the electromagnetic spectrum. To put that in perspective, if the electromagnetic spectrum were the length of a football field, the visible light we perceive would be about the width of a human hair. Think about it: we see 0.0035% of what's right in front of us. But hey, let's keep acting like we totally understand what's going on around us and keep arguing about it on the internet. In the same way, our perception of sound is a tiny part of a larger reality. It's like being invited to the symphony of the universe but only hearing one triangle ding, from the parking lot. You get the point—what we can see and hear is ridiculously minuscule. If we see and hear that little, imagine comparing what we do know to what we don't know. It's humbling, to say the least.

Quantum physics has revealed that Reality is far more mysterious and interconnected than we once thought. It challenges our conventional assumptions about space, time, and the nature of matter. At the subatomic level, particles behave in ways that defy classical understanding. They appear and disappear, exist in multiple places at once, and respond to being observed.[1] They exhibit a fluidity that challenges our linear thinking. If fluid and dynamic principles govern the material world, why should we assume that miracles are unnatural? We're missing the bigger picture when we see them as deviations that violate the laws of nature.

Jesus demonstrated mastery over these unseen kingdom principles. He operated in a way that revealed a higher Reality . He had a deep understanding of the interconnectedness of all things, and the power of intention to shape the physical world. His miracles, whether walking on water, healing the sick, or multiplying food, weren't performed as magic tricks. You don't need a VIP backstage pass to the Throne Room or a platinum-level prayer membership. There's no divine frequent flyer program. Miracles are for us all.

They weren't isolated events designed to impress or entertain people but were signs of how the kingdom of God operates. He demonstrated the power of faith and the potential for human beings to access the divine realm and live as kingdom citizens. He never treated miracles as rare or weird interruptions but as a natural outflow of God's life within and around Him.

In John 14:12, Jesus made a fantastic statement that is a challenge to our limited thinking and an invitation to embrace a lifestyle of extraordinary possibility: "Very truly I tell you, whoever believes in me will do the works I have been doing, and they will do even greater things than these" (John 14:12 (NIV). When Jesus said that, He wasn't giving us a quote for a motivational poster. He was pointing toward a deeper Reality where the supernatural isn't an interruption. Instead, it's how things work when you're living in sync with the divine pattern. If miracles were meant to be a rare exception, isolated incidents reserved for a select few, why would He say that his followers would continue them and even do even greater ones? His statement suggests that miracles aren't limited to a chosen few but are accessible to everybody who believes.

RETHINKING THE SUPERNATURAL

The term "supernatural" implies something beyond nature, something foreign to our reality. It suggests a separation between the natural and the divine. But if God is the Creator of all things, the source of all existence, then miracles aren't interruptions of natural law but expressions of a more complete Reality. The early church understood this and recognized the potential to access God's power and to manifest His kingdom on earth. The apostles regularly experienced healings, visions, and divine interventions, not as once-in-a-lifetime moments that defied explanation, but as a way of life. For them, miracles were the natural outflow of their connection to the Father of Miracles.

Acts 5:12-16 describes how people would bring the sick into the streets so that even Peter's shadow might fall on them and heal them. This wasn't treated as extraordinary; it was simply what happened when the divine life of Christ flowed unhindered through a person aligned with that Life. The supernatural was their natural. It was a testament to their faith and deep understanding of the interconnectedness to God and, for that matter, to all things.

The question, then, isn't whether miracles are real or possible within our current understanding of Reality but why we have stopped expecting them. Have we lost sight of how Reality functions and given in to a limited materialistic worldview that restricts our potential for experiencing the miraculous? I suspect most have.

The Role of Expectation in Miracles

One of the most overlooked yet necessary elements of experiencing miracles is expectation. Our beliefs give rise to our expectations, and what we expect (faith) shapes our perception, and our perception fashions our reality. In the Bible, Jesus repeatedly emphasized the necessity of faith, highlighting the power of belief to influence outcomes. He told the woman with the issue of blood that her faith had made her well, verifying the role of her unwavering belief in her miraculous healing. He reminded his disciples that if they had faith, even the size of a mustard seed, they could move mountains. This is a clear lesson on the power of even small amounts of faith to overcome seemingly insurmountable obstacles.

Science has shown us that expectation influences reality in profound ways. The placebo effect, for example, demonstrates that people's belief in a treatment can lead to fundamental physiological changes in their bodies. If belief can alter biological functions, it stands to reason that it could also be a key in tapping into the miraculous and unlocking the potential for extraordinary outcomes. Belief literally connects us to the power of God in a way that changes things in life.

Consider how often Jesus asked people if they believed before performing a miracle. He didn't need their faith to work wonders. However, their faith did act as the bridge between unseen potential and physical manifestation. It allowed them to experience the connection between the natural and supernatural. The same spiritual principle is true today.

Expanding Our Perspective on Miracles

Modern physics has revealed that time and space aren't as fixed as we have believed. This growing knowledge of the quantum world has changed our linear and deterministic view of the universe. The past, present, and future are connected in ways we are only beginning to understand.[2] This connection suggests that actions in the present can influence both the past and the future. For instance, does God's forgiveness take away sins from our past as if they never happened? Every believer knows that is the case. The Bible is clear about this. In Christ, your old life is gone. Not just "forgiven" but replaced. You've been given a new past. You've been "in Him before the foundation of the world." So yes, God does retroactive miracles. He's the only One who can edit your backstory and still call it the truth. That's great news for us all but especially for those who have memories of "a past" they wish wasn't theirs. Good news: it's not. Your past is *in Christ*.

This lines up with the biblical instances where supernatural intervention often transcends human limitations of time and space. Faith connects us to the potential for divine power to operate beyond the constraints of our conventional understanding. For example, in the healing of the paralytic in Mark 2, Jesus forgives the man's sins and tells him to pick up his mat and walk. Was this simply a physical healing, or was something deeper going on here? Looking at this miracle through the quantum lens suggests that Jesus was tapping into an unseen reality where the man was already whole and, through faith, collapsing that eternal Reality into his space/time present moment. Can you see how it was a demonstration of the power of divine intention to transform the physical body and the past traumas that may have contributed to his condition?

Living with an Expectation of Miracles

If miracles are meant to be normal, how do we begin to realign our thinking and experience? It all seems so foreign, even weird. How do we actively cultivate a mindset of faith and expectation and step into a reality where the miraculous becomes a natural part of our everyday lives? The first step is shifting our perspective from one of separation to one of integration inside our union with God. Instead of seeing the supernatural as something outside of ourselves because God is up there and we are down here, we must recognize that we are already one with Him and are part of a miraculous reality called "the kingdom of God." We have to see that we possess the potential to manifest extraordinary outcomes through the power of our faith.

Remember, your faith is His faith that He gave to you. The Apostle Paul said it well: "The life that I now live in the flesh, I live by the faith *of* the Son of God" (Galatians 2:20, KJV, emphasis added). You don't need more faith. You have all you need, but what you may need is to know the truth that already exists.

Paul wrote in Romans 12:2, "Do not conform to the pattern of this world, but be transformed by the renewing of your mind." That's not a religious suggestion. It's a neurological instruction. Change your thinking, change your wiring, change your experience.

The way we think about miracles affects how we experience them. If we expect them to be isolated incidents reserved for special circumstances, that will be our reality. But suppose we begin to live with an awareness that God is always at work on our behalf, that miracles are a natural expression of the power and love of God? When that happens, we open ourselves to greater possibilities by allowing the miraculous to manifest in our lives.

Jesus didn't just perform miracles; He revealed how the universe operates at its highest level. He showed us the potential to transcend the physical world's limitations and operate from a place of divine power and purpose. Science is only now catching up to what faith has long proclaimed: that reality is shaped by belief, that all things are connected, and that unseen forces influence what we call the material world.

The question isn't whether miracles still happen but whether we are willing to expect, see, and participate in them. Suppose we shift our mindset and embrace a perspective of faith, expectation, and union with God and His kingdom. When we do, we will discover that the supernatural has been natural all along. We'll see that miracles aren't unusual but a fundamental facet of our Reality, waiting for us to awaken to their presence and embrace their transformative power.

As we move through this book, will you resolve to step into a life of extraordinary possibility, where the power of the Divine is readily accessible and where the miraculous becomes a regular part of your everyday experience? You'll become convinced that you don't need more faith. You don't need to "try harder." You don't need to get more religious and start talking King James English.

You just need to remember. Remember who you are. Remember what He said. Remember what's already true. The supernatural is your native language. You've just been speaking doubt with a religious accent because you didn't know better, but that can change.

This requires a conscious intention to challenge limiting beliefs, cultivate a heart of gratitude and expectation, and align with the divine frequency of love, compassion, and unwavering faith. As we each embrace this integrated perspective, we can become agents of transformation and manifest the kingdom of God on earth. We have the opportunity to make Christ's imminent presence known, and live the life we were created to know and enjoy.

Chapter 3

Faith and Physics: Partners in the Miraculous

We're not in the Middle Ages anymore. We've got particle accelerators, the Hubble telescope and now the Webb telescope that has found *more* galaxies. Not planets—*galaxies.*

Not to mention quantum physicists quoting spiritual mystics without even flinching once. And somewhere in the background, I can imagine God smiling, whispering, "Took you long enough."

The Enlightenment period ushered in an era of scientific reasoning, emphasizing empirical evidence and dismissing anything that couldn't be measured or tested. By its nature, the supernatural fell outside the scope of scientific inquiry. Over time, this led to the widespread assumption that miracles were either violations of natural law or nothing more than superstitions.

But know this: the Creator of gravity, DNA, and dark matter doesn't get rattled when somebody asks for empirical evidence. As Einstein said, "Science without religion is lame; religion without science is blind." Max Planck, the man who opened the door to this whole quantum science journey said there's a conscious and intelligent mind behind the energy holding everything together.

That's not a science-vs-God statement. That's science staring directly into the mystery and saying, "Okay, maybe there's more going on here than atoms and equations." The day when science and faith often opposed each other is gone and this is a new day. Unless, you're still clinging to the old science of materialism. If the pioneers of quantum physics saw no contradiction between science and faith, we seriously need to rethink this false dichotomy.

THE EVOLUTION OF SCIENTIFIC UNDERSTANDING

Science itself has undergone radical shifts in understanding over the centuries. The science you and I grew up with isn't much older than three centuries and, to some degree, it has seen its day. I don't mean to suggest it's all wrong because it certainly is not. It has been, however, short-sighted, but that is changing. Science is supposed to change. That's the whole point. Growth isn't possible without change.

The new quantum science proves that what was once considered mystical or supernatural often became explainable through scientific discovery. Disease was once attributed only to divine punishment or demonic activity but is now understood in terms of biology and genetics. God is helping us to grow so that we know better and then do better.

If history teaches us anything, it's that the unknown shouldn't be dismissed as impossible because we don't understand it. The miracles described in the Bible don't contradict natural law but reveal a level of natural law that we don't fully understand. What if the supernatural only looks that way because it's unfamiliar?

Just as technological advancements have allowed us to harness unseen power in areas such as electromagnetism, spiritual principles like faith and intention allow us to engage with unseen forces in ways science is only beginning to explore. Trust me, science will never catch up with God, but it's exciting to see it moving forward in discovering the divine truths that have always been there.

QUANTUM PHYSICS AND THE MYSTICAL NATURE OF REALITY

One of the most surprising revelations of modern physics is that reality is not as fixed as we once believed. Quantum mechanics has shown that particles can exist in multiple states at once (superposition) and that observation influences the behavior of matter. As we'll explore more deeply in Chapter 6, this principle, known as the observer effect, may hold the key to understanding how faith interacts with unseen possibilities. These findings defy the classical Newtonian model of a deterministic universe that operates like a machine. They open the door to possibilities that align perfectly with the miraculous potential God has embedded in this world.

Consider Jesus' ability to heal from a distance, walk on water, and multiply food. It's my contention that He was actually operating within laws of Reality that we are only now starting to grasp. Quantum mechanics shows us that reality is influenced by observation and intention. Is it possible that faith manifesting as focused intention acts as a catalyst that brings unseen possibilities into tangible form? As we will see, that is absolutely the case.

The Role of Consciousness in Shaping Reality

Quantum physics and neuroscience agree: your mind isn't just a passenger—it's a driver.[1] The double-slit experiment shows that your observation changes outcomes. (I explained what has been called "the experiment that broke reality" in my book, *Quantum Life*.) That's not some weird woo-woo; it has been peer-reviewed in many scientific journals.

Jesus wasn't spouting motivational soundbites when He said, "According to your faith, be it done unto you." He was describing how the system works and modern neuroscience backs Him up. Placebo studies show that belief alone can trigger actual healing in the body.[2] Thoughts aren't just private reflections; they're chemical cocktails, vibrational frequencies, and creation tools. Faith isn't wishful thinking. It's Reality's steering wheel.

This concept is repeatedly seen in Scripture, where Jesus often emphasized the need for faith to see miracles manifest. "According to your faith, let it be done to you" (Matthew 9:29). If observation can change the behavior of particles, is it so far-fetched to believe that faith (expectant observation) plays a big role in shaping our reality?

JESUS AND THE PHYSICS OF MIRACLES

Throughout the Gospels, Jesus performs miracles that challenge the perceived limitations of reality. When He turns water into wine, He demonstrates mastery over transformation at a molecular level. When He calms the storm, He shows authority over nature. When He heals the sick, He demonstrates a profound understanding of energy, vibration, and human biology.

The disciples often struggled to understand Jesus' miraculous actions because they were caught in a classical, materialistic worldview. But Jesus operated from a different perspective, one that saw reality not as fixed and unchangeable but as fluid, dynamic, and responsive to divine intention. "With

God, all things are possible" (Matthew 19:26) isn't just a statement of faith; it also reflects the underlying nature of Reality itself.

Bridging the Gap Between Science and Faith

If science and faith are complementary, we should expect more evidence of their convergence as our understanding grows. In recent years, studies on prayer and meditation have demonstrated measurable effects on the brain, immune system, and even external events. Prayer changes the brain. That's not up for debate anymore.

For instance, research conducted by Dr. Herbert Benson at Harvard University shows that meditative prayer significantly reduces stress and enhances physiological well-being.[3] Experiments in consciousness research, such as those led by Dr. Dean Radin at the Institute of Noetic Sciences, suggests that human intention can influence physical outcomes in measurable ways: science processes and records how faith, prayer, and affirmation of eternal principles in our world change things.[4]

In other words: you're a walking, breathing bundle of consciousness who can shape outcomes, rewrite internal programming, and literally tap into unseen dimensions of divine power. Philosopher Pierre Teilhard de Chardin eloquently stated, "We are not human beings having a spiritual experience. We are spiritual beings having a human experience." What an exciting time to be alive!

LIVING AT THE INTERSECTION OF FAITH AND SCIENCE

Throughout history, saints, mystics, and prophets' lives have given us countless testimonies of miraculous interventions once considered ordinary in their context. St. Teresa of Ávila experienced mystical visions that today might be analyzed through the lens of consciousness studies. In my own study of her writing, especially *Interior Castle*, I've marveled over how ahead of her time she was in experiential knowledge. Meister Eckhart taught about the profound interconnectedness of all things, giving principles then that now are validated by quantum entanglement.[5]

As those who want to move into the miraculous, we need to explore this intersection with curiosity rather than fear. The more we understand the nature of Reality, the more equipped we are to walk in the miraculous. Science isn't just catching up with Scripture. It's helping us see how the truth works.

The challenge we face is to be open-minded and seek truth wherever it can be found. We need to recognize that science and faith are both partners that can guide us toward a greater understanding of how we can tap into these divine laws God has established. Don't let a religious background cause you to dismiss what science has to say. God is the God of actual science, too. And it's time we stop treating science like a threat and start treating it like an ally.

When we open ourselves to the One who promised to guide us into all truth (John 16:13), we just might discover that the boundary between science and the supernatural isn't as solid as we once thought. Instead, it is a bridge that connects the seen and the unseen, the mysterious and the miraculous. It joins our experience in life with the power of God in ways we haven't known until now.

LET'S KEEP GROWING

We stand on the precipice of a new era, where what was once considered impossible is becoming demonstrably real. As we continue on this journey, let's keep our hearts and minds open toward embracing the unity of science and spirituality. To do this will equip us to grow closer to grasping the hidden mysteries of existence.

As science continues to unfold the mysteries of our universe, a pattern emerges that reveals striking parallels between modern scientific discoveries and ancient spiritual teachings. Quantum physics, in particular, has demonstrated principles that used to be exclusively reserved for spiritual, mystical traditions. When we open our minds, we will see our understanding of miracles in a way past generations could never have imagined. God invites us into an expansive vision where the miraculous is the norm. Embracing this vision causes the boundaries between science and faith to blur into a beautiful expression of divine truth.

For example, studies on quantum entanglement conducted by physicists like Anton Zeilinger have shown us that two particles separated by a great distance remain connected in a mysterious relationship.[6] His concept reminds us of the spiritual idea of interconnectedness taught by Meister Eckhart and other mystics. The Apostle Paul said the same thing in his way when he wrote, "For in him all things were created: things in heaven and on earth, visible and invisible, whether thrones or powers or rulers or authorities; all things have been created through him and for him. He is before all things, and *in him all things hold together"* Colossians 1:16-17 (NIV, emphasis added).

Cutting-edge neuroscience is another discipline that has provided compelling evidence that practices such as meditation, prayer, and mindfulness alter our mental state and physiological health. They bridge the gap between physical reality and spiritual experience. According to neuroscientist Dr. Andrew Newberg, author of *How God Changes Your Brain*, regular engagement with spiritual practices literally reshapes our neural pathways and enhances our capacity for empathy, compassion, and resilience.[7] This strongly echoes the experiences described by many spiritual leaders throughout history. "Let this mind be in you, which was also in Christ Jesus," may have more significant implications than we have recognized. His mind affects our brains.

Then there is epigenetics, the field pioneered by Dr. Bruce Lipton. It demonstrates that beliefs and perceptions directly influence genetic expression, supporting the biblical teaching that belief profoundly impacts physical reality. The bottom line is that science today is no longer simply validating spiritual concepts; it actively reveals the deeper structure of reality itself. It's a reality where consciousness, intention, and faith are inseparable from the very core of our existence.

The Bible consistently affirms the profound power of belief, just as Jesus validated when He said, "If you have faith as small as a mustard seed... nothing will be impossible for you" (Matthew 17:20). This scriptural promise strongly resonates with findings in quantum mechanics and consciousness research. Both highlight the idea that reality is malleable, shaped actively by observation, intention, and expectation.

Physicist Amit Goswami reinforces this point too, suggesting consciousness is fundamental to reality, not simply a byproduct of material existence.[8] These kinds of insights challenge the outdated idea that spirituality and science exist on opposing ends of a spectrum. Instead, they intersect in a dynamic way, constantly informing and nurturing each another. As the false division dissolves, a richer understanding emerges. We are able to embrace both a scientifically credible and spiritually profound view of the world. With each passing decade, scientific progress affirms the teachings of the Bible, transforming spiritual truths into measurable phenomena. Instead of diminishing our sense of wonder, these discoveries amplify the awe and reverence we feel when we consider God's design in creation. In merging science and spirituality, humanity stands poised on the brink of a new era, one not defined by division but by unity, coherence, and a shared exploration of the miraculous potential woven into the very essence of reality itself.

As faith opens its arms to science, and science opens its eyes to mystery, something holy is happening. This science isn't about proving God. He doesn't need that, but it is about partnering with Him. The boundaries between heaven and Earth, seen and unseen, science and Spirit, are dissolving like sugar in southern sweet tea.

And the invitation is still there: Come taste and see.

CHAPTER 4

THE MECHANICS OF MIRACLES

We understand miracles as supernatural phenomena beyond natural law, attributed to divine action or unexplainable powers beyond human knowledge. But as scientific knowledge expands, especially in quantum physics, what was miraculous may prove to fit well with the nature of a divine reality greater than what we had understood. All these findings are giving us a new perspective for understanding the miracles of Jesus and supernatural events as documented in Scripture. Thanks to science, we find ourselves shifting away from a naive definition of miracles as violations of natural law to a more spiritually sophisticated concept of them as manifestations of another order of Reality. Science is elevating our perspective so that we are seeing more of the divine order in the miracles.

Theoretical physicist Amit Goswami, has extensively discussed the relationship between quantum physics and spirituality. In his book *Science and Spirituality: A Quantum Integration*, Goswami argues that the paradoxes of quantum physics can be resolved by considering a spiritual universe that demonstrates a metaphysical unity between science and spirituality. He goes so far as to say that the idea that consciousness is the ground of being is the basis of all spiritual traditions. His work highlights the connection between consciousness, a central concept in quantum physics, and spirituality.

MIRACLES AND THE QUANTUM WORLD

At its center are principles seeming to reflect the nature of miracles in the Bible and defying the deterministic, linear nature of how we've conceived of the world. Who would have thought that science would come along expanding our ability to grasp faith's power and reality's nature?

There are many but let's consider a few:

1. Superposition – Quantum particles are in many places all at once until observed. They exist in a realm of possibility waiting to become actualized. We see then that reality isn't absolute and fixed but holds infinite possibilities. Your future can change because focused faith can bring the impossible into the possible. As Jesus said, "With man this is impossible, but with God all things are possible" (Matthew 19:26). When you function from the mechanics of miracles as God has designed it, you can throw away the word "impossible" because God/Ultimate Reality doesn't respect that word.

2. The Observer Effect – The observation causes a quantum state to collapse into a definite state, demonstrating the active role consciousness has in creating reality.[1] It implies that where you set your attention has a role in determining reality. The phenomenon points toward how faith serves as an observer effect that causes unseen possibilities to manifest into physical reality. Maybe it's the reason Jesus insisted on faith first when He performed miracles. Expectation was a factor in the miracle happening. It shows how what we believe and expect has the potential to transform the world by working as a catalyst for change. Changing your focus charges your faith.

3. Quantum Entanglement – When two particles are entangled, their state instantly becomes linked regardless of how far away from each other they are. Distance has nothing to do with it.[2] This can help us understand how people were healed by Jesus from a distance, as with the centurion's servant (Matthew 8:5-13). It demonstrates how intention can transcend physical space. It also implies how grace and faith potentially affect reality across space and time, weaving a matrix of oneness that defies common sense. Faith isn't concerned with distance. Your thoughts, your prayers, and your focus can affect people and situations even though you aren't near them. Be careful how you think and talk even when you aren't in the midst of the situation because these things matter.

JESUS' USE OF QUANTUM PRINCIPLES

Jesus showed a profound grasp of reality beyond what was His disciples could understand. He was working from a Reality above and beyond the physical limitations in this world. At one point, He told them He wasn't able to say many things to them because they wouldn't understand it. (See John 16:12.)

- **The Multiplication of Bread and Fish** – When Jesus multiplied food to feed the 5,000, He didn't cause food to come into existence where none existed. What He did was to multiply what was already present in the unseen realm. It was there all along. It's a good illustration of abundance in the spiritual realm, where the potential reality was brought into space and time by faith. We could reasonably conclude He was accessing an unlimited source of divine supply and illustrated faith's ability to bring it into experience in spite of what looked like scarcity. That explanation certainly fits with what science currently teaches us. *See* it then see it.

- **Curing the Sick** – Jesus cured with a touch or a word. Quantum biology proposes that the body works on an energy level and frequencies and vibration control health. Modern medicine proves this by using frequencies for healing in several proven ways, from physical to neurological to speculative energy-based methods. Clinically accepted tools like ultrasound (1–3 MHz) and TENS Units (1–200 Hz) use mechanical or electrical frequencies to reduce pain, improve circulation, or break up kidney stones. Neurological therapies like transcranial magnetic stimulation (TMS) and PEMF modulate brain or cellular activity with magnetic fields to treat depression or stimulate tissue repair.[3]

I've used it. Family members have used it. Friends have used it and, clearly, Jesus used it then. By working at a divine frequency, He was able to resonate people's bodies with wholeness instantly, balancing their energy system back into harmony.

THE PLACE OF CONSCIOUSNESS IN MIRACLES

One of the world's deepest realizations from quantum physics is that physical reality is shaped by consciousness.[4] It contradicts traditional notions of causality and indicates that our thoughts and beliefs physically influence the world we experience around us. Jesus taught faith, awareness, and believing as requirements of miracles, and He underscored the role of human consciousness in determining our reality.

I wrote about possible realities as an endless number of air bubbles floating in an ocean of possibilities in my book *Quantum Life*. Being directed in faith toward a certain result affects which bubble pops and drops into your reality. If you want to see a particular outcome "pop and drop" into your life, change your focus. See the outcome as if it has already manifested.

Jesus described the Kingdom of God as something already present but needing awareness to see (Luke 17:21). If reality is created by consciousness, and we learn to see the love of God in all our circumstances, we can change the world we experience from being limited to miraculous possibility. Through greater awareness of ourselves as connected with God through Christ, we may discover our ability to experience miracles in day-to-day life.

Broadening Our Definition of Miracles

Through our exploration of faith and quantum science, we're able to understand miracles no longer as unpredictable acts of God but as the inevitable consequence of participating in the higher order of reality inside the Kingdom of God. Learning Kingdom culture doesn't take away from their amazement; it increases our ability to take part in them, enabling us to become participating co-creators with God. It doesn't reduce the role of miracles in life but enhances it by inviting us all to participate.

By accepting both scientific discovery and spiritual truth, we unlock deeper faith, increased expectation, and a life filled with the miraculous as a natural reality. Through this shift in how we perceive what is possible, we are equipped to live more with purpose and intent.

HISTORICAL PERSPECTIVES ON MIRACLES AND SCIENCE

Great thinkers and religious leaders throughout history have tried to blend science with miracles, trying to grasp those underlying principles that govern nature as well as the supernatural world. The early church fathers, such as Augustine and Aquinas, examined the philosophical underpinnings of miracles. More recently, scientists such as Sir Isaac Newton and Blaise Pascal had profound religious faith while believing their findings simply disclosed God's universe's complex design. They believed that science can increase appreciation for God's handiwork in this world. So, to them science nurtured faith.

Outside of Christianity, cultures and other religious traditions have documented supernatural events that look like quantum realities. Buddhist monks have slowed their rate of body metabolism and controlled body temperature through meditation. Indigenous shamans discuss energy fields and healing modalities similar to contemporary theories in quantum biology.[5] All this implies a more universal quality about miracles than we've thought. It seems almost silly to point out that God's goodness transcends religion and cultures. The way He has created reality to function isn't unique to Christians. God is good to everybody. The law of aerodynamics works for all of us. Everyone flies on an airplane because that's how God created it. He makes it "rain on the just and on the unjust" (SEE MATTHEW 5:46). Everyone's crops require rain, and that's what God provides.

PRACTICAL APPLICATIONS: LIVING WITH A MIRACULOUS MINDSET

If miracles are inherent to reality, how can we adopt a mindset consistent with them? How can we take an active role in embracing the mechanics of quantum physics and spiritual truth in order to unlock human potential to experience miracles in day-to-day reality?

Consider these practices:

1. Intentional Observation – Where we direct our awareness makes a difference if observation affects reality. Reflecting on the promises of God, imagining results in line with trusting His goodness, and giving thanks can all serve to direct awareness so miracles can occur. Start being aware of using only positive, empowering thoughts, and feel thankful for blessings all around you.

2. Tuning in to Divine Frequency – If Jesus healed by vibration and resonance, then tuning into the divine frequency becomes a pathway to experiencing the miraculous.

"Tuning into divine frequency" is just another way of saying "abiding in Christ" or "walking in the Spirit."

Grace is so big that God offers these miraculous blessings for all people, even unbelievers. Don't take issue with that statement. Paul wrote, "Or do you show contempt for the riches of his kindness, forbearance, and patience, not realizing that God's kindness is intended to lead you to repentance?" (SEE ROMANS 2:4) Yes, God pours out His grace on us all.

3. Expectation and Boldness – Time after time, Jesus encouraged his disciples to expect miracles. Living with bold faith implies taking a step forward in expectation and doing what Truth directs and not being held back by the logic of our minds. Question your assumption of what can or can't happen and adopt a mindset of unlimited possibilities.

4. Non-Local Prayer and Intercession – If quantum entanglement implies we are all connected on a deeper level, then prayer is no longer bound by space and time. Research on prayer has revealed beneficial effects even when patients aren't told they are being prayed for.[6] This supports what Jesus said: "Whatever you ask for in prayer, believe that you have received it, and it will be yours" (Mark 11:24). Make a habit of praying over others with intention and concentration, and imagine the healing and change occurring even as you pray.

Miracles as a Higher Form of Natural Law

I hope by now it is already apparent to you how miracles aren't acts of magic or sporadic deeds of where God interrupts the normal flow of life. No, they are manifestations of living inside His Kingdom. Quantum physics has revealed to us a glimpse into Reality's fabric, and its workings are in line with Jesus' actions and teachings. The more we discover these parallels, we will discover miracles aren't suspending natural order but fulfilling it on a different plane.

By changing our awareness, coming into harmony with the Mind of Christ, and living with expectation, we become capable of experiencing miracles in our lives. The quantum mechanics of miracles challenges us not only to believe but to become participants. We are to walk in the Reality that was demonstrated by Jesus, where faith isn't only believing but is the very energy that creates the world we experience.

We are called to move into this world with wonder, not with fear. The more we know about the nature of reality, the more prepared we are to see the miraculous. Instead of seeing science as a challenge to faith, we can see it as a channel that carries us to a better understanding of how God works. It is not a call to forego critical thinking but to push beyond what we know now and welcome more knowledge.

The challenge in front of us is to keep an open mind, seek truth wherever it leads, and to see science and faith as both roads to a deeper appreciation of the way God works. If we take this approach, we may discover that the line between science and the supernatural isn't as fixed as we imagine. It's a bridge between the seen and the unseen, the known and the mysterious, and the possible and the miraculous. It's an invitation to welcome mystery and discover the unlimited possibilities of a universe where faith and science are joined together.

CHAPTER 5

PRAYER IS ACTION AT A DISTANCE

From faith healers to shamanistic rites, the human experience abounds with accounts of people overcoming illness and injury through seemingly supernatural means. Remember that these are God-fashioned laws of nature that span everything and everybody's belief systems. "Are you suggesting that even people who don't trust Christ can experience miracles?" you may still wonder. Yes, I am. Our Loving Father is so good that He is willing to do wonderful things even if He doesn't get credit for it immediately. One day, they will see, but in the meantime, human confusion doesn't thwart His goodness. I knowingly reaffirm this truth because it contradicts what many Christians have wrongly believed.

One of the most fascinating aspects of Jesus' healing ministry was his ability to heal from a distance. He didn't always need to lay hands on somebody or even be physically present for them to experience healing. This aligns with a concept in quantum physics known as non-locality, where objects can be instantaneously affected by one another across vast distances. As physicist Nick Herbert observed, "Non-locality is the universe's way of winking at itself."[1] By the way, don't be offended when somebody says "universe" instead of "God." Whether they know it or not, they are pointing to the Source of all miracles. Every good and perfect gift comes from God, even if they don't know it.

JESUS AND NONLOCAL HEALING

One of the most straightforward and compelling examples of nonlocal healing in Scripture is the story of the Roman centurion's servant (Matthew 8:5-13). The centurion, recognizing Jesus' authority, told him, "Just say the word, and my servant will be healed." Jesus commended the centurion's great faith, and at that very moment, the servant was healed, even though Jesus never physically saw or touched him. This story highlights the power of belief and the potential for healing to occur regardless of physical proximity.

This pattern is seen several times in the Gospels:

> Jesus healed the daughter of a Canaanite woman from
> a distance (Matthew 15:21-28). Despite the geograph-
> ical distance, the woman's persistence and unwavering

faith caused Jesus to extend his healing power to her daughter.

He declared the healing of an official's son in a different town (John 4:46-53). The official's trust in Jesus' word was enough to bring about the healing of his son, demonstrating the power of belief to transcend space and time.

He healed the ten lepers simply by giving them instructions, and as they walked away, they were cleansed (Luke 17:11-19). Their obedience to Jesus' instructions activated their faith and allowed them to experience the miraculous healing of their leprosy.

Another vivid demonstration of nonlocal healing is in Jesus' encounter with the Syrophoenician woman who had gone to Jesus on behalf of her demon-possessed daughter. The child wasn't even in her presence. No physical touch. No Hollywood scene. Only conversation and a word of confirmation.

Jesus praised the faith of the woman and, without taking even one step forward, assured her daughter's healing. She arrived home to discover that her child was totally restored. This is another instance when time, space, and distance wasn't an obstacle to faith's power.

From the quantum viewpoint, this miracle again shows how distance makes no difference in outcome, and intentionality (particularly based on trust) changes physical reality. The lady's intention and absolute faith became the connection point for divine power to physical healing even in unseen space.[2]

These accounts suggest that healing isn't limited by physical proximity. If God's power operates beyond space and time, our understanding of healing must expand beyond the conventional cause-and-effect paradigm we've lived with all our lives. We must consider the possibility that healing can occur through nonlocal means, influenced by causes such as faith, intention, and the interconnectedness of all God's creation to Himself.

THE SCIENCE OF NON-LOCALITY

Quantum entanglement refers to a physical phenomenon in which two particles, once entangled, are still connected no matter how far apart they are. If one of them changes its state, the other immediately matches this change, even if huge spaces are between them. Albert Einstein called this "spooky action at a distance," because it appeared to challenge conventional physics as he had understood it.[3] Quantum entanglement implies a greater reality where space and time are not what we have thought they are.

This scientific reality mirrors the way prayer and faith seem to function. Studies on intercessory prayer have shown that patients who are prayed for, even without their knowledge, often exhibit better recovery rates than those who are not. While skeptics dismiss these results as placebo effects, quantum physics suggests that human consciousness and intention may have measurable effects on physical reality. These effects aren't fully understood, but they point to the potential for nonlocal connections to influence health and well-being. Larry Dossey, MD, a pioneer in exploring the relationship between consciousness and healing, wrote in his book, *One Mind: How Our Individual Mind Is Part of a Greater Consciousness and Why It Matters*, "Nonlocal mind implies that everything is potentially connected to everything else." What is this nonlocal mind of which he speaks? It is the all-encompassing presence of the Divine Love that fills everything.

If quantum entanglement suggests that all things are interconnected at a fundamental level, then faith could be the force that bridges the gap between the seen and unseen. Faith isn't simply blind belief but rather a confident assurance based on spiritual understanding and a deep trust in the power of God. The Bible describes faith as "the substance of things hoped for, the evidence of things not seen" (Hebrews 11:1). Faith may act as an unseen thread that connects the physical and spiritual realms, allowing divine energy to flow where it is directed.[4]

Jesus frequently highlighted faith as vital to receiving healing:

"Daughter, your faith has made you well.

> Go in peace and be freed from your
> suffering." (Mark 5:34)

> "If you have faith as small as a mustard
> seed, you can say to this mountain,
> 'Move from here to there,' and it will
> move." (Matthew 17:20)

> "Everything is possible for one who
> believes." (Mark 9:23)

This suggests that faith is more than a mental mindset. It's not a feeling but a force that influences outcomes, in the same way observation in quantum mechanics determines a particle's state. Our belief system shapes our reality, and unwavering faith can unlock the potential for miraculous healing.

Prayer as an Energetic Transmission

Prayer is often viewed as a conversation with God but is much more than that. It also serves as a form of energetic transmission. If human consciousness can influence reality in the way quantum experiments suggest, then prayer might function as a focused intention that affects people and circumstances beyond physical limitations. Prayer is not just a passive request but an active engagement with the power of God. Pay close attention to that fact: Prayer is more than *asking*. It is *action* that activates divine power.

This concept isn't restricted to religious contexts. Research into meditation and intention has proven that group meditation reduces crime in cities, stress, and even affects distant recipients' biological processes. The evidence implies collective consciousness (the mind of Christ that fills the cosmos) can literally change what's going on in the world around us. Can you see how prayer is a manifestation of this principle? Prayer is an effective way of harnessing divine energy and bringing healing to people and communities.

HEALING AS AN ENERGY SHIFT

Many miraculous healings could be explained through the lens of energy transformation. The body is composed of electrical and magnetic fields, and disruptions in these fields are often associated with illness. Traditional Chinese Medicine, for example, emphasizes the importance of balancing Qi, the vital energy that flows through the body. Jesus' healing may have involved restoring balance to these fields, aligning them with divine wholeness. That's not some woo-woo New Agey thing so don't discard this if you heard it there first. It's science. Jesus may have been able to channel divine energy and restore harmony to the energetic systems of those He healed. Don't be turned off by using language that isn't a biblical vocabulary. It's all God at work.

Consider this biblical evidence:

- **Touch as a Conduit of Power** – To heal the man who was born blind, Jesus spat on the ground and mixed the water from his spittle to make mud. He put it on the man's eyes. Then he told him to wash in the Pool of Siloam. The action might sound weird, but in it is hidden an important principle: physical matter, coupled with intention, became a conduit for divine healing.

This wasn't magic. It was a synthesis of physical touch and spiritual awareness. Jesus utilized physical elements to act as a carrier system for spiritual energy. From a quantum sense, matter is energy contained in physical form, and intention can mold it. In this instance, healing energy wasn't just spoken but was transferred through physical means.

Current studies in energy medicine have confirmed that touch is capable of changing physiological levels. The biblical practice of the laying on of hands has scientific underpinning. And what Jesus showed us in physical terms, science is now testifying to energetically.

- **Words as Vibrational Commands** – Jesus often healed simply by speaking. If words carry vibrational energy, then His voice certainly carried healing frequencies that restored wholeness to the body. Our words have the power to create or destroy, and Jesus' words were infused with healing energy that could transform the physical body.

- **Resonance and Alignment** – Just as one tuning fork can make another resonate with the same vibration, can you understand how Jesus' presence made people resonate with divine wholeness? His presence generated an energy field that encouraged healing and wholeness in those around him. (Remember, you also possess that same Energy.)

Engaging Nonlocal Healing in Our Lives

If healing isn't bound by time and space, we can participate in nonlocal miracles today. How can we actively engage with the power of faith and intention to bring healing to ourselves and others? Here are practical ways to engage:

- **Pray with Focused Intention** – Just as Jesus declared healing from a distance, we can expectantly pray for others, believing that our prayers transcend physical location. Approach prayer with unwavering faith and visualize the healing taking place. That visualization is nothing less than faith at work.

- **Speak Life-Giving Words** – Words possess energy. Speaking health and wholeness over ourselves and others can align with divine realities. Use your speech to inspire, uplift, and bless those who are around you.

- **Align with Divine Frequency** – Through worship, meditation, and embracing the promises of God's unilateral goodness toward those He loves (all of us), we can attune ourselves to higher spiritual frequencies that promote healing. Immerse yourself in practices that consciously connect you to this Divine Love and strengthen your sense of inner peace and well-being.

- **Develop Absolute Trust** – To Jesus, faith was always associated with healing. The greater we condition ourselves in believing in miracles based on God's goodness, the more conducive we are to an environment of miracles. Challenge and reject your negative thoughts and welcome the chance of phenomenal results through the mental shift you embrace.

- **Practice Gratitude and Expectation** – Gratitude resonates as a powerful vibration aligning us with divine abundance. Instead of doubting, expecting healing creates channels for divine energy to flow. Practice having a heart full of gratitude and expect to witness God's blessings unfolding in your life. Thankfulness paves the way.

- **Agreement in Prayer and Collective Faith** – The Bible teaches that miracles happen when two or more agree in prayer (Matthew 18:19-20). Quantum experiments show that collective focused attention amplifies intention. Connect with others in prayer and intention, knowing that your collective energy will amplify the power of your requests. I'll never forget the day our Grace Walk Experience online community stood in agreement that a pulmonary embolism in my wife's lung would dissipate. To the doctor's amazement, it went away overnight. "We must've been wrong," the doc said. Yeah. Right.

- **Laying Hands on the Sick** – Although healing can occur from a distance, Jesus also used touch. Scientific studies confirm that physical touch releases oxytocin and enhances immune response.[5] Use physical touch, when appropriate, to convey compassion and support.

HEALING THROUGH TIME AND DISTANCE

Non-locality doesn't only apply to physical space but also to time. Some people experience healing by addressing past emotional wounds or generational trauma. While the concept of "generational curses" misses the mark because Jesus has broken every curse, it is the case that the past may be affecting our present circumstances. However, this suggests that divine healing is not constrained by our linear perception of time. As with distance, time doesn't stand in the way of healing when we see the truth.

Might prayer about past situations bring healing into the present? Could faith reach into the future, affecting possibilities yet to come? The Scriptures provide this option to us when, in Mark 11:24, Jesus refers to asking and receiving as if it has already occurred. It challenges us to think of cause-and-effect in new terms and implies there must be some way in which past situations can still be affected by intention.

Nonlocal healing challenges our traditional view of reality, but both quantum physics and biblical accounts affirm that distance and time are no obstacles to God's healing power. If everything is connected at a fundamental level, faith and prayer may be vehicles for transmitting healing energy across any distance and even our past experiences. Jesus operated within this reality effortlessly and invited his followers to do the same. By understanding the principles of faith, intention, and divine connection, we can step into miraculous healing where physical limitations no longer apply. As we embrace the potential for nonlocal healing, we open ourselves to a world of extraordinary possibility and become agents of transformation in the lives of others.

CHAPTER 6

FAITH SPEAKS AND REALITY LISTENS

One of the deepest findings in quantum physics that breaks old paradigms is the observer effect. It's the principle that observation affects the behavior of particles. This surprising idea challenges how we usually think about reality—it suggests that just by looking at something, we actually change it.[1] The possibilities in a world where reality is seeming to bend to what we put our attention are mind-blowing. Once again: faith and miracles are magnified by where we put our focus.

Where are you looking? Toward a good outcome or a bad outcome? Think about the implications of the way faith, expectation, and perception become key factors in creating the outcomes we receive. Faith functions as a lens by which we can alter the very fabric of our reality. The Bible consistently teaches faith as receiving from God, and this new science is beginning to illuminate why and provide thrilling insights into the ability of consciousness to impact the physical world.

Understanding the Observer Effect

In the famous double-slit experiment I described in *Quantum Life*, scientists observed that light and electrons could behave as particles and waves, depending on whether or not they were being watched. This dual nature of matter challenged classical physics, which assumed that objects had definite properties independent of observation. We thought they were the same whether we were looking or not. Science proved (repeatedly) they aren't.

However, when the researchers attempted to measure or observe the phenomenon, the particles "chose" a definite state. This suggests that observation collapses the field of possibilities into a single outcome. In other words, reality exists in potential until it is observed. It's a vast sea of probabilities waiting to be actualized. Outcomes aren't set in stone, as materialistic science and legalistic religion have often suggested. As theoretical physicist John Archibald Wheeler famously said, "No phenomenon is a phenomenon until it is an observed phenomenon."[2] This highlights the crucial role of not anticipating a negative outcome based on what we can see. We need to look beyond the temporal into the transcendent Kingdom of Kindness to bring divine reality into our lives.

If this holds true in the physical realm, it stands to reason that it can hold true for the spiritual realm as well. Faith becomes the observer effect manifesting, creating realities unseen into tangible form. Faith speaks the word and then reality does the work. Can you see how believing unambiguously in a certain result can actually alter the very nature of reality? James said it clearly: ""But let him ask in faith, nothing wavering" (James 1:6). The Bible teaches, "Faith is the substance of things hoped for, the evidence of things not seen" (Hebrews 11:1). This is very similar to what we see illustrated in quantum physics: reality as a field of infinite potential until observed or believed into existence. Our faith serves as a conduit between the invisible world of possibility and reality as we know it. Don't dwell on the negative possibilities. Ask for a result based on God's goodness instead. The change in your mindset contains more inherent power than you've yet to discover.

JESUS AND THE OBSERVER EFFECT

Again and again, Jesus illustrated the force of observation and faith and their ability to impact the physical world. The miracles were not sporadic acts of divine interference but illustrations of a principle in action—the ability of faith to condition reality.

- **Curing the Blind Men** – In Matthew 9:27-30, Jesus questioned two blind men if they believed He was capable of doing this. They affirmed their faith, and He replied, "According to your faith, let it be done to you," and they were cured. Their faith in Him doing this was what brought about the divine energy necessary for them to feel its effects.

This miracle wasn't just an arbitrary act of divine action but seemed to be influenced by the person's expectation, focus, and faith. Their observation and what they believed to be possible determined the outcome.

SHIFTING REALITY THROUGH BELIEF

If our expectations (faith) shape reality, cultivating the right mindset becomes imperative for experiencing the miraculous. If we believe miracles are possible, we open ourselves to the potential for experiencing them. Jesus continually emphasized the importance of faith, sometimes even rebuking his disciples for their doubt.

When they failed to cast out a demon, he told them, "Because of your unbelief... Truly I tell you, if you have faith as small as a mustard seed, you can say to this mountain, 'Move from here to there,' and it will move" (Matthew 17:20). This shows that faith functions as an activator, collapsing the unseen potential into reality. If we doubt, we collapse the possibility of failure. In that moment, we use negative faith and point in the wrong direction. To the contrary, if we believe, we collapse the possibility of success in the outcome.

The link between faith and physical manifestation permeates throughout the Bible:

Mark 11:24 – Believe that whatever you ask for in prayer, it will be yours, and it will be so.

James 1:6-7 – But when ye ask, ye must believe and not doubt, because he who doubts is like a billow of the sea, blown and cast about by the wind.

2 Corinthians 5:7 – For we walk by faith, not by sight.

HOW SCIENCE SUPPORTS THE POWER OF BELIEF

Research has repeatedly shown that belief has tangible effects on the body and mind, providing scientific validation for the power of faith to shape our reality.

- **The Placebo Effect** – Patients who are convinced that they are receiving effective treatment will actually improve, even after receiving a sugar pill. This proves that expectation by the mind can impact physical health, illustrating the strong link between mind and body.

- **Neuroplasticity** – The brain can rewire itself based on thoughts, beliefs, and repeated focus. This suggests that what we consistently observe and expect shapes our reality at a biological level. By consciously focusing on positive and empowering thoughts, we can reshape our brains and create new neural pathways that support our goals and aspirations. It's the grace space where amazing things happen.

- **Research on Positive Expectation** – Successful athletes visualize success. People who anticipate favorable results are more likely to achieve them. This illustrates how visualization and positive expectation can determine performance and results.

Dr. Masaru Emoto's water experiment showed how spoken words and intentions impact water molecules, causing its molecular structure to change in either a symmetrical, lovely pattern when using positive statements or a chaotic, unorganized form when using negative statements.[3] Since human beings are primarily composed of water, this implies that what we say and what we believe may literally mold reality itself.

These findings confirm what Jesus taught: belief is not a passive state but a force that shapes reality. Our thoughts, emotions, and beliefs have a tangible impact on our physical and spiritual well-being.

Aligning with the Miraculous

If this observer effect holds true with faith, we must pay attention to what we're focusing on. "All that you can see," God told Abraham, "Is what I will give you." We must make a concerted effort to think with faith and expectation, aligning ourselves with miracles becoming a reality in our lives.

Here are ways we can align with the miraculous:

- **Guard Your Mind** – Negative expectation brings about negative realities. It's negative faith in action. Instead, think about faith-filled realities. Keep your mind guarded against negativity and actively think about positive and powerful thoughts. Ignore naysayers, but pay close attention to the One whose heart's desire is to see you blessed.

- **Speak Life** – Jesus often spoke miracles into existence. Our words shape what we experience. Use your words to affirm the truth of God's promises and to declare the reality you want to see manifest.

- **Visualize and Trust Miracles** – If faith is evidence of unseen realities, then envisioning success resonates with divine possibilities. With a sanctified imagination, envision vividly your desired outcomes and solidify your faith that those are realizable.

There's no instrument more powerful than a sanctified imagination.

- **Surround Yourself with Faith** – Jesus removed doubters from the room before raising Jairus' daughter from the dead (Mark 5:40). Stay around people who reinforce belief. Seek out relationships with people who encourage and support your faith journey.

- **Affirmations on a Daily Basis** – Reciting faith-filled statements reprograms your brain according to divine truth. (For instance, "I walk in God's favor. Miracles are normal in my life.") Reprogram your subconscious mind by using affirmations and strengthen your faith in your success and prosperity potential.

The quantum physics observer effect creates a scientific analogy of Jesus' lesson on faith. The reality we perceive is based on what we observe, believe, and anticipate. If aligning with divine truth causes miracles, faith isn't something optional but is what unlocks the supernatural. When faith speaks, reality listens and acts.

By turning your mind toward expectation instead of doubt, you bring God's unseen potential into reality. Just as a scientist influences what happens in an experiment by observation, so do we form our lives by what we decide to believe. Faith isn't a wishy-washy sentiment. It's an active force that controls the unseen and actualizes divine realities into personal experience. It's an important step towards embracing the authority of your faith and entering into a life of unhindered possibility, where miracles are a normal occurrence of your daily experience.

Chapter 7

Tuned In To Christ Consciousness

Tuning in to God isn't about earning approval from Him but discovering the proper frequency. Precise dialing is necessary with radio to pick up a clear signal, just as accurate alignment is needed of our thoughts, attitudes, and beliefs with the frequency of divine truth. Doubts and fears will interfere with reception by creating spiritual static, but when we tune in with faith and love we come to resonate with the mind of Christ. And in that state of inner harmony, miracles don't happen through forced effort. They naturally play out in life.

Throughout the Bible, we see a strong emphasis on the importance of aligning ourselves with the mind of God. This is more than an intellectual understanding. It is a deep, intuitive knowing that reaches further than the limitations of human reasoning. It is the state of being in synch with God's thoughts and ways as we allow His life to flow through us in such a way that our union with Him animates our thoughts and actions. Or, to use another New Testament phrase, we are "walking in the Spirit" at that place.

Quantum mechanics and neuroscience reveal that coherence, or the harmonious alignment of our energy and intention, plays a critical role in shaping reality.[1] As quantum physicist Max Planck stated, "Science cannot solve the ultimate mystery of nature. And that is because, in the last analysis, we are a part of the mystery we are trying to solve." To experience miracles necessitates getting on the wavelength of grace. The mystery of miracles can't be solved inside legalistic logic that looks for formulas to produce them. We have to tune into God's way of doing things. That requires we abandon any notion that miracles are earned and instead see that they are *embedded* in life itself. Get your mind right and you'll get your life right.

When Jesus performed miracles, He demonstrated the power of quantum coherence, where His thoughts, emotions, and faith were perfectly synchronized with the mind of His Father. Miracles manifested as a result of that coherence. In fact, without it, they wouldn't have happened. Jesus once said, "Very truly I tell you, the Son can do nothing by himself; he can do only what he sees his Father doing because whatever the Father does, the Son also does" (John 5:19, NIV). The expression of His coherence with the Father enabled Him to perform miracles. Could the renewal of our minds bring us into coherence with the Kingdom Way so that we, too, will experience the miraculous? Could it be that simple? Yes, it is. The simplicity of faith was what Jesus alluded to when He said we need to become like little children.

What is Quantum Coherence?

From a scientific standpoint, quantum physics sees coherence when particles, waves, or fields of energy are in harmony and in synchronization with each other. Think of a well-tuned orchestra with each instrument sounding in harmony with each other, producing a beautiful and strong sound. A system becomes more powerful, stable, and efficient when it's coherent. The energy runs in a smooth and efficient manner, enabling the system to become highly functional. On the contrary, when a system's coherence fails, it becomes inefficient, fractured, and unstable. The energy gets dispersed and wasted, causing a decrease in its power and efficiency.

This principle applies to everything from lasers to biological systems to human consciousness. Neuroscience and quantum biology studies suggest coherence improves efficiency, health, and function. The entire organism benefits when cells communicate effectively and work together in harmony. In the same way, heart coherence where the heart's electromagnetic field synchronizes with brain waves, has been linked to increased mental clarity, emotional resilience, and physical well-being. The HeartMath Institute has demonstrated that coherent heart rhythms are associated with improved cognitive function, reduced stress hormones, and enhanced immune response.[2]

From a spiritual perspective, coherence can be understood as relating to Christ in a way that brings us into alignment with Him and the way He does things. It's the grace space where faith, thought, emotion, and action exist in perfect harmony with God's Reality. It's a state of being where our inner world aligns with the will of God, allowing us to become conduits for divine power. Jesus embodied this state completely, demonstrating how alignment with His Father leads to supernatural power. His life was a testament to the power of coherence, showing us what is possible when we fully align ourselves with God's purpose.

Go With the Flow

Hungarian psychologist Mihaly Csikszentmihalyi, in his work on "flow states," highlights the power of focused attention and complete absorption in an activity to unlock extraordinary potential. His work reminds me of what many have called "flowing in the Spirit." He wrote, "When we are involved in [flow], we feel that we are living more fully than during the rest of life." Doesn't that sound like being tuned in?[3] His research into flow states provides a psychological and scientific framework that mirrors the principles of faith, deep spiritual engagement, and even miraculous manifestations taught in the Bible. He suggests that flow is a state in an activity where time seems to disappear, the effort becomes effortless, and a person operates at their highest potential.

Jesus often demonstrated a deeply present state of faith that acts beyond fear and self-consciousness. It's what occurs when we are so intently fixed on God and immersed in goodness that everything else becomes secondary to us. Here's how Csikszentmihalyi put it: "A person in flow is completely focused. There is no room for self-doubt or anxiety about failure."[4] In his book *Flow: The Psychology of Optimal Experience*, he identified a number of flow characteristics deeply in line with what the Bible teaches about miracles and faith:

Complete Concentration on the Present Moment

With flow, there isn't room for doubt or hesitation in the mind. It's what the Bible describes as having single-minded faith (See Mark 11:23). It's what James was writing about when he said, "But when you ask, you must believe and not doubt" (James 1:6). The nature of flow state is your external condition becoming saturated with the all-encompassing awareness of God's love. Spiritual coherence results when we recognize our union with God.

A Sense of Effortlessness and Timelessness

Csikszentmihalyi's model proposes that actions run naturally without stress when people are in flow. Do you see how this meshes with grace-based faith as demonstrated by Jesus? One where we don't struggle but simply rest in Him?

Miracles aren't the result of struggling for an outcome but of resting in complete knowledge of God's goodness. "Come to me, all you who are weary... and I will give you rest"

(Matthew 11:28). Grace empowers us to live as if life is a rest, not a test. Jesus didn't give us some sort of religious regiment to perform miracles. To Him, the supernatural is simply a more expansive understanding of the natural inside His Kingdom.

Loss of Self-Consciousness and Fear of Failure

Self-doubt dissolves in Csikszentmihalyi's description of flow state; he surrenders to the activity and becomes it. He isn't concerned about himself but assumes automatically that everything will turn out as it should. He stated, "The psychic entropy of worry is replaced by the ordered experience of flow."[5]

It's also true of faith. Miracles occur with ease, and fear doesn't come (SEE MATTHEW 8:26) because we are resting in God's perfect love. "Perfect love casts out fear" (1 John 4:18). There's no need to hype some religious activity to a frantic fevered pitch. It's simply a matter of resting in the ordained way our loving Father has designed this miracle matrix to function.

Flow, Faith, and Quantum Mechanics

Just as quantum mechanics reveals that observation and intention shape reality, Csikszentmihalyi's research suggests that deep focus and intention bring breakthroughs. He explained, "When we are in flow, we are fully immersed in what we are doing, we lose our sense of self, and we feel a deep sense of satisfaction."[6]

That's an accurate description of resting in Christ. It's the way faith causes unseen realities to manifest into physical reality. His psychology research very much follows what the Bible has to say about what it appears like when we "flow in the Spirit," trusting God has our best interests in mind as part of His plan. You don't need to "make it so." Coherence creates a calm assurance that "it is finished" even when you haven't yet perceived it.

Jesus and Quantum Coherence: Miracles as Divine Alignment

The miracles of Jesus are a classic illustration of quantum coherence with God, where the flow of reality was reshaped by a convergence of faith, intention, and the Father's plan. Consider these illustrations:

- **The Feeding of the Five Thousand (Matthew 14:13-21)** – As previously discussed in Chapter 4, Jesus accessed a quantum principle here. His coherence with the Father put Him on the frequency for miracles to occur. When Jesus multiplied the loaves and fish, he first gave thanks. Gratitude increases coherence in the heart and mind, raising our frequency to a state of expectancy and faith. His ability to see abundance where others saw lack influenced the field of possibility and collapsed Reality into a state of supernatural provision. His gratitude shifted the energy and tuned into the abundance of heaven.

- **Healing by a Word (Luke 7:1-10)** – The centurion was aware of the principle of authority and agreement. He knew that if only the word was spoken by Jesus, the miracle would take place. The faith he commended was also about how faith and congruence with divine reality move beyond physical limitations. The centurion's grasp of authority stemmed from a profound trust in divine alignment's power.

- **Walking on Water (Matthew 14:22-33)** – Peter initially stepped into the miraculous, walking on water as long as he was tuned into Christ-consciousness. The exact moment fear entered his consciousness and disrupted his internal coherence, he began to sink. This demonstrates that maintaining a state of divine alignment is key to sustaining the miraculous. Peter's experience illustrates the importance of staying tuned into Christ and trusting Him in challenging circumstances.

- **The Transfiguration (Matthew 17:1-8)** – The face and apparel of Jesus radiated divine light in a way that may well have signified a state of complete quantum coherence. If light and matter are interwoven on a fundamental level, it makes sense that Jesus was functioning from a vibrational frequency that caused his physical body to reflect his divine nature. His experience indicates humans may have the ability to transcend their physical bodies in a way that brings Light to every situation they encounter. Some people just "light up the room." You can be that person.

The Science of Coherence and Consciousness

Neuroscience and quantum biology reveal that coherence in the mind and body produces extraordinary results, suggesting a deep connection between physical and spiritual well-being. Research at the HeartMath Institute shows that when heart rhythms and brain waves synchronize, people experience heightened intuition, reduced stress, and increased healing capabilities. This coherence is a physical phenomenon that reflects emotional and mental well-being.[7]

Studies suggest that focused observation stabilizes quantum states.[8] In other words, what we consistently focus on becomes reality, reinforcing the biblical principle that "as a man thinks in his heart, so is he" (Proverbs 23:7). Our thoughts shape our reality, and consistent focus on specific outcomes can lead to tangible results. Where we put our attention is the station where we dial in.

Neuroplasticity

The brain has a natural ability to rewire itself according to habitual thought patterns. When Paul writes of "renewing the mind" (Romans 12:2), maybe he was unknowingly writing about a process of aligning neural paths with divine reality. Through focusing intentionally on beneficial and empowering thoughts, we can mold our brains and form new neural paths conducive to the goals and dreams we desire.

The Placebo Effect

Numerous studies reveal that just believing can cause physiological changes. If expectation can heal, how much more can abiding faith in God's goodness, not a placebo but Reality, achieve miracles? The placebo effect shows us the potential of the mind to effect change in the body, illustrating faith's potential to trigger healing processes in us. If a sugar pill can trigger change, think about how the gospill (gospel) of the kingdom can change a person's life!

ACHIEVING QUANTUM COHERENCE: THE MIND OF CHRIST

How do we enter into a conscious awareness of mystical union with God? How do we access the "mind of Christ" and tune into its full potential? Paul teaches us that we already possess the "mind of Christ" (1 Corinthians 2:16). But experiencing it needs deliberate practice and dedication to aligning thoughts, emotions, and actions with divine truth, and there's nothing legalistic about it.

1 Timothy 4:7 instructs us to "exercise thyself rather unto godliness." (KJV) The Greek term for exercising (*gumnazó*, from where we derive the word "gymnasium") implies studious, disciplined training, just as an athlete trains a physical body. You and I are invited to train a spiritual body toward godliness.

Following are some exercises to tune into the Christ-Frequency:

- **Meditate on Divine Truth** – Consistently dwelling on God's goodness and your identity in Christ reinforces harmony with divine reality. In over 50 years spent counseling people, a lack of understanding authentic identity has been, by far, the greatest debilitating hinderance I've seen with clients who are struggling with life. Tuning into our identity in Christ is the solution. "Faith comes by hearing, and hearing by the word of God." (Romans 10:17). The Word of God is more than scripture. It is Christ. Sink into Him and let His indwelling Life change your mind and heart.

- **Speak with Authority** – Jesus spoke healing, peace, and miracles into being. Words create reality. "Death and life are in the power of the tongue" (Proverbs 18:21). Speak your words to establish the reality of God's promises and declare the reality you want to see become real. Stop complaining. You're cursing yourself when you do that. Psychologists talk about "self-fulfilling prophecies" so don't prophesy something if you don't want it.

- **Regulate Your Emotions** – Inner harmony creates physical and spiritual balance. Prayer and meditation tune the mind, body, and spirit. Take this approach to control your emotions and purposefully connect with God's peace and love. People who allow their emotions to rule them will only find what they want when they learn to control their emotions instead of being controlled by them. Don't say, "I can't help it." You can. Christ lives in you and will empower you.

- **Walk in Love and Oneness** – Love is the highest vibration. Jesus taught us to love because divine energy flows through relational harmony (John 13:34). Have relationships based on love, compassion, and solidarity. When you've tuned into Love, you are on the exact frequency where miracles happen.

- **Practice Stillness and Silence** – Amidst a world full of noise, stillness tunes your inner self with divine awareness. "Be still and know that I am God." (Psalm 46:10) Develop mindfulness and meditation to still your mind and listen to the still, small voice inside. Don't talk so much when you pray. Take some time to sit still, set your attention on God's love and just wait.

It's in that stillness that God speaks clearest.

Quantum coherence can scientifically explain supernatural ability demonstrated by Jesus and those who follow Him. When faith, thought, and action are congruent with divine reality, then reality conforms to God's will and heart. Scripture teaches that a renewed mind can change things, and science shows us that coherence in awareness creates amazing breakthroughs.

The concept of Christ-consciousness is not some theological abstraction but an invitation to operate on a higher plane of awareness. Through the development of spiritual coherence, we tune into a frequency where miracles are real and anticipated. When hearts, minds, and spirits are in harmony with divine truth, we bring about the supernatural as natural reality in our lives. Therein lies the mystery and power of the Kingdom of God working in us. As we adopt precepts of quantum coherence and build a life of alignment with divine reality, we can realize our full potential and become agents of change in society. This is the melody of heaven, calling us to a life of purpose, power, and possibility not known until now.

Chapter 8

The Energy Field of Miracles

Faith is more than belief. It's energetic alignment with divine reality. Like every object in the universe, you and I are vibrational beings, continuously broadcasting and receiving signals. Scripture identifies it as living in the Spirit. Science identifies it as resonance. Either way, the principle remains the same: by aligning ourselves to God's love and truth, we find ourselves in a frequency in which miracles occur. Not because we've done anything to deserve them, but because we're now tuned to the field in which they're already available in abundance. This phenomenon called the "law of resonance" accounts for why some prayers seem to break through and others seem to bounce back, and how synchronizing ourselves to the force of God's kindness establishes us to experience the miraculous.

Religious traditions over the centuries have described the potential embedded in union when we consciously align with God and with His will. It's not only Christianity which identifies with this necessity. From Samadhi among Hindus to Nirvana among Buddhists to Wu Wei among Taoists to Tawhid among Muslims, the search towards living from union with God is common. This universal desire for a conscious relationship with God indicates that we were made to experience union with Him. Not just theoretically or even simply objectively, but *experientially* to know union with God. Being a believer in Christ, I am convinced He is the door to experiencing that reality.

The modern science of quantum mechanics teaches us that everything in the universe operates at a frequency. Zoom in close enough to any physical matter, and you'll reach a place where you find pure, vibrating energy at its core. This Law of Resonance states that frequencies naturally synchronize with others at the same level. A radio receiver tuned to a particular frequency will pick up a station broadcasting at that same frequency.

In a comparable way, we need to align our internal frequencies with God if we want to experience and manifest His favor. As Nikola Tesla so eloquently put it, "If you want to find the secrets of the universe, think in terms of energy, frequency, and vibration." Not just science's secrets but also faith's. The question to us is, "Who's energy? What frequency? Which vibration?" I hope you are seeing all those are in Christ and His kingdom.

If miracles operate within the vibrational fabric of reality, then miracles aren't random occurrences but the result of what happens when we adjust our human experience with the divine frequency of the Kingdom. It's a matter of dialing in to the heart of God. Be very clear on this point: The broadcasting signal of God is pure love.

The idea I want you to see is that it's only when we fully perceive God as loving, kind, gracious, and generous that we get clear reception of the "miracle frequency." Those who think God is distant, aloof, judgmental, and punitive won't see miracles very often because their perception of Him puts them off frequency. It's not that God isn't willing. It's just that they aren't tuned in. They are locked in to a caricature of God —a false god and so aren't in position for miracles. To say it another way; they're tuned to AM (Adamic mentality), while miracles are broadcast on FM (faith mentality). An Adamic mentality is the old mindset from Adam. It's limited, fear-based, and rooted in separation. It operates from lack and logic. Faith mentality, on the other hand comes from Jesus. It flows from union, confidence, and trust in divine love.

In this Land of Love, God has created miracles not as rewards of our doing good but as expressions of His goodness. All we need to access these miracles is to resonate with a heart of love like His own. Knowledge about resonance and its relationship to universal principles throws a profound light on how we actively engage in the miraculous and transcend a state of passive expectation to an active co-creation of divine reality.

EXAMINING THE LAW OF RESONANCE

Resonance takes place when a vibrating system causes another system to adopt its frequency. It can be seen with musical instruments. When a tuning fork is struck, another tuning fork of the same frequency close to it will also start vibrating without actually having come into contact with it. The first tuning fork transfers energy to the second, so it resonates in sympathy with it. Comparably, in quantum physics, particles and waves become synchronized when both are in an exactly similar state of energy. Synchronization isn't a sporadic thing but a natural property of everything in the universe. This scientific concept has deep spiritual connotations. Jesus often mentioned what could today be termed as resonance:

"Seek first the kingdom of God and His righteousness, and all these things shall be added to you." (Matthew 6:33). It's about resonating correctly. Seeking God's righteousness means getting on the same frequency as Him and to operate in the divine flow. When we do that, "all these things" are the natural outcome. We don't strive for righteousness but step into it. We don't force faith; we flow in trust. We don't manufacture miracles. Instead, we adjust our frequency to the reality where there already are.

Jesus' teaching in Matthew 6:33 encourages us to relax, tune in, and allow miraculous energy to flow effortlessly. Chill out. God is on our side! We are blessed with divine synchronicity, effortless faith, and miraculous living. "I and the Father are one" (John 10:30). That statement by Jesus reveals an in-depth grasp of interconnectedness, not only about His connection to the Father, but ours too.

Jesus' life modeled how He was completely online with His Father. It was because He was fully attuned to the vibration of divine energy so that He was able to perform miracles and move above physical limitations. Being in a state of unshakeable faith and total reliance on God's plan and the indwelling Spirit of God, He was able to become both a receiver and broadcaster of divine energy. As resonance drives energy interaction in the universe, think about what will happen when you tune into this same miracle-working energy that played out in the life of Jesus. It's through accepting His love that we become resonant with miraculous energy. Will you tune into the frequency of Divine Life, source of all miracles, and then let them take place in your own life? You don't manufacture miracles. You manifest them.

JESUS AND RESONANCE: MIRACLES AS A FREQUENCY SHIFT

Jesus' miracles involved bending reality as most understood it. At times it happened when sickness turned to health, lack turned to plenty, and impossibility became possible. He could alter the vibrational frequencies of his environment and create conditions for transformation. Just like Jesus, *you have the ability to bend daily reality* to match Divine Reality.

Look at these examples of this with Jesus:

- **Healing the Sick** – His presence seemed to recalibrate those who came into contact with him. A person can't meet Jesus and not be changed. Just as a healthy tuning fork causes a misaligned one to vibrate correctly, Jesus' perfect divine frequency restored people's bodies to wholeness. His compassion and unwavering belief in their potential for healing created a resonant field that activated their innate healing abilities and brought them to where they could receive. He adjusted their perspective until they believed.

You have that same ability. The Bible affirms it: "And if the Spirit of him who raised Jesus from the dead is living in you, he who raised Christ from the dead will also give life to your mortal bodies because of his Spirit who lives in you" (Romans 8:11, NIV). Same Spirit, same outcomes.

- **Calming the Storm** – When Jesus rebuked wind and waves (Mark 4:39), He imposed a higher vibration of peace on the turbulent elements and resonated them into agreement with His will. Words had a vibrational energy broadcast by Him that quieted down the storm, proving how words can impact the physical world. Do you have storms in your world that need to be calmed? Take note and start speaking in faith.

- **Multiplication of Food** – When Jesus multiplied the loaves and fish (Matthew 14:13-21), He drew from an unseen frequency of abundance. He was tapping into a station broadcasting from inside the kingdom of God. The power of faith then manifested abundance even in the face of scarcity. Nothing may be on the plate, but there's plenty in the Kitchen. Many reading these words could attest to that being proven repeatedly in their lives.

- **Turning Water into Wine** – Because the vibrational structure of molecules determines their state, Jesus was able to alter the frequency of water to become wine. This transformation shows that matter is not irrevocably fixed and can be changed through the divine power to which we have access. Let's not deny it just because we can't fully make sense of it. I utilize a lot of things in life although I can't fully understand how they work—my car, electricity, computer, cell phone and a million other things. I use them because I know the one who designed and made them have ensured they work. And the more I used them, the more confidence I have in their reliability. Should we trust God any less?

Jesus performed miracles as a man who relied on His Father at work, bringing amazing outcomes that defied material explanation. How does this apply to your life? In greater ways than you can imagine. Ask the Spirit of Miracles who lives in you to guide you into interpreting, appreciating, and applying this faith phenomenon in your life.

THE POWER OF WORDS AND VIBRATIONAL ALIGNMENT

We know that science has shown that sound and words carry vibrational energy. Studies like those previously mentioned by Dr. Masaru Emoto on water molecules demonstrate that positive words create structures that show harmony, while negative words generate chaotic patterns.[1] These experiments suggest that our words have a tangible impact on the physical world, influencing the vibrational frequencies of matter. Jesus demonstrated this principle repeatedly:

- **Speaking to the fig tree** – Jesus cursed the tree, which withered (Mark 11:12-14, 20-21). His words carried an energy that caused the tree to quickly decay and die. You, too, can bring an end to some things you have been asking God to end. Have you considered that while you've been asking Him, He may be asking you to do it?

- **Testifying in pronouncements** – He spoke, and people were healed (Luke 17:12-14). The energy of healing was in His words and restored wholeness to those who were sick. It's a gift to meet people who bring help and hope in times of dark periods in life. Be such a person.

- **Power of Blessing and Cursing** – Jesus taught that our words hold creative or destructive power (Matthew 12:37). Our words can shape our reality and influence the lives of others. Bless yourself and others. Don't complain; instead, confess that God is God and God is good—always.

- **The Centurion's Servant** – Jesus healed from a distance simply by declaring the outcome (Matthew 8:5-13). His words transcended physical limitations, demonstrating the non-local nature of divine power. The frequency of His words resonated with the situation at a distance. What a difference it makes when we change our words about troubling situations. Remember, your words can trigger outcomes, so choose them carefully. Fearful, negative words will resonate with the same sort of outcome. Faith-filled words that express the goodness of God in challenging circumstances will resonate with a similar outcome.

If the universe is responsive to frequency, then words of faith spoken in tune with Divine Love can serve as waves that carry miraculous change. Our words aren't just sounds but vibrational forces that can shape our reality and influence the world around us.

Some may remember the 1970s TV ad that demonstrated how Ella Fitzgerald's singing voice was so powerful that it broke a glass. Our voices contain energy with the potential to change situations![2]

How to Align with Divine Resonance

Have you seen how the key to experiencing miracles lies in coming in to resonance with God's frequency? How can we cultivate this alignment and unlock our potential for manifesting the miraculous? Here are some practical steps:

- **Renew Your Mind** – Align your thoughts with divine truth. Scripture says, "Be transformed by the renewing of your mind." (Romans 12:2). Challenge your limiting beliefs and replace them with empowering truths that line up with the thoughts of Christ. Repent of every lie you've believed about miracles. Reject the notion that you aren't worthy of a miracle, that miracles are extremely rare, or that you don't have enough faith. Ask the Spirit to show you lies you have believed. Then, reject them and replace them with the truth that God loves you and is more than willing to always act in the way that is for your highest and best.

- **Surround Yourself with the Right Frequency –** To get your mind in order, establish a space conducive to your growth as a spirit and keeping your mind focused on God's love for you. Quit listening to sermons telling you how terrible you are. You've been made "the righteousness of God in Him" (2 Corinthians 5:21). Quit begging God to change you and, instead, ask Him to make you see yourself as He sees you—a masterpiece. (See Ephesians 2:10) Quit promising to try harder and trust Him, knowing if He "did not spare his own son, but gave him up for us all —how will he not also, along with him, graciously give us all things?" (Romans 8:32)

- **Avoid Lower Vibrations** – Doubt, fear, and negativity lower spiritual energy. Remain in a position of faith, expectancy, and hopefulness. Shield yourself from influences that undermine your faith and thwart your potential. It may occasionally even require avoiding situations or people that consistently pull you down. Guard your inner state of peacefulness. *It is up to you to guard you.* There's no selfishness in taking care of yourself. As they say during airplane safety briefings, "Put your own oxygen mask on first so that you may assist others more effectively." You can't help others if you aren't secure. Don't feel guilty about putting your well-being first even when it means doing something others may not appreciate or understand.

- **Engage in Deep Meditation and Contemplation** – Repeating this in numerous chapters in this book is intentional because it is so very important. Spiritual meditation will attune your consciousness to the awareness of Christ in you and amplify resonance with God's will. Practice mindfulness and create space for quiet reflection and contemplation. Don't constantly talk to God. Be still and listen. He wants to speak to you, too. Sometimes the most helpful word you may hear is, "Shhhh!"

- **Align Your Actions with Faith** – Faith isn't passive, but an active force that motivates towards action. According to the Bible, "Faith without works is dead" (James 2:26). Don't just wait idly, expecting something to magically shift; become a part of the reality of your faith. Live as if your desired result already exists (i.e., see it with the eyes of faith). Experience it in your heart. Talk about it with confidence. These purposeful actions not only build your faith—they align your mind, heart, and spirit with the reality you want, making it real even before it comes to full manifestation.

Miracles are the natural byproduct of aligning with the divine truth inside God. Jesus was a perfect resonator with God's frequency and invited others to join him in doing the same. Through knowledge of the Law of Resonance, both biblically and scientifically, as well as through implementing it by faith, by word, and by purposeful aligning, you can nurture an environment where the miraculous becomes ordinary. When Jesus healed certain blind men, Matthew 9:29 (MSG) records, "He touched their eyes and said, 'Become what you believe.'" Wayne Dyer wrote: "You get what you vibrate." Same thing from two different voices.

When we live, believe, and speak in harmony with divine reality, we step into the energy realm of faith—a vibrational plane in which the miraculous has become normal. There, we are no longer pleading for miracles or looking for special cases. We are in resonance with the very vibrations that make them a done deal. Just as tuning forks ring in resonance with their equals, our spirits harmonize with the heart of God when we live in faith, trust, and divine expectation. This is the call of faith: to pass from passive believing to an active co-partnership with the Creator, where heaven pours through us, and miracles are no longer shocking, but simply the way things are.

CHAPTER 9

THE SUPERPOSITION OF FAITH

Faith asks us to live in a paradox: fully engaged in earthly life while, at the same time, anchored in heaven. It's not denial but divine tension. Quantum physics describes the phenomenon as superposition and refers to the bizarre state of particles in several states at the same time, until observed.[1] The Bible describes it as "walking by faith, not by sight." Both refer to the same deep underlying reality: that more than one reality is at work.

In Christ, we sit in the heavenly sphere while we still move through earthly challenges. The issue isn't that one realm is the so-called "real" one and the other isn't. As previously discussed, the issue revolves around which one we're tuned in to. Faith in no way discounts the realities of this world; it does see beyond the temporal into the Reality of God's kingdom. And when we look with eyes of faith, we bring to the earthly experience the reality of eternity. It's then that miracles happen.

Picture a coin spinning in mid-air—its heads or tails until it lands. That's a fair example of a quantum particles in a state of probabilistic fuzziness, a state of possibilities, until it encounters a conscious observer. It's weird, I admit it. When I first learned about this new science, I thought it was nutty, but it's been demonstrated again and again and again. Physicist Michio Kaku said it best: "It is often stated that of all the theories proposed in this Century, the silliest is quantum theory. Indeed, some say that the only thing that quantum theory has going for it is that it is undoubtedly correct."[2]

The idea that two seemingly contradictory things can be true seems strange to the rational mind. We tend to think in binary terms, concluding that it has to be "this" or "that." There's little space in linear thinking to recognize that it could be both. But the same dilemma exists inside faith too.

Consider the example mentioned already. The Bible says you are seated with Christ in heaven. (SEE EPHESIANS 2:6). You know you are here, on this earth, inside time and space. "You are in the world," says John 17:11. So, which is it? Am I here? Am I there? Yes.

Many other biblical truths like this are paradoxical. They seem to contradict each other, but they are both true. That's the quantum world for you. The kingdom of God is a different culture that plays by different rules. No wonder God said, "My thoughts are not your thoughts, neither are your ways my ways" (Isaiah 55:8). Sometimes it just makes no sense. That's true in faith and science.

When one of the founders of quantum mechanics first began to study the paradox of it all he said, "One who is not shocked by quantum theory has not fully understood it." The Bible says spiritual truth is "foolishness" to the natural mind. Then it's true in science and faith.

Superposition means that anything is possible and that sometimes both are true. I'm in the world. I'm in heaven. I'm sick. I'm well. I'm in need. I lack nothing. I'm weak. I'm strong. The list goes on and on. When we look at the temporal world of circumstances, we see one set of facts, and when we look at the transcendent world of Christ, we see a truth that may seem to contradict those facts. Both are valid. What we experience depends on where we put our attention (prayer) and what we expect (faith). Your miracle already exists in superposition inside what I've previously refered to as "Reality" with a capital R but now I think I'll call it REALITY. After all, God's REALITY deserves all caps, don't you agree? Think of REALITY as the eternal realm in contrast to this temporal, lowercase world of "reality." It's just a matter of it manifesting in your spacetime reality.

Science and the Bible teach us that infinite possibilities exist for us because temporal reality exists inside eternal REALITY. (Science calls it "the field".) The act of observation collapses those possibilities into a single, tangible outcome. It's not only that we don't know the state of the particle until it manifests; the fact is that it doesn't *have* a final state until we measure (observe) it. Will your prayer be answered? Well, think of it this way: It has already been answered in eternity. Do you see the answer? The answer to your prayer has already been done according to what God knows is the very best outcome for you, whether you see it in your situation yet or not. But it will manifest. Oh, yes. It surely will. On that, you can depend. *See it "before you see it."* Then go ahead and sign off on it in faith and watch what God does.

The Bible describes a kingdom principle where some things are "already but not yet," where spiritual REALITY exists prior to its full manifestation in natural reality. The Kingdom of God is both present reality and yet a future expectation to be fully executed. Jesus resided in this tension between earth and heaven and illustrated how faith works in quantum superposition. The unseen and seen coexist in an it-is-finished answer until faith causes one possibility to become concrete reality.

Jesus acted from a place of divine goodness, even in situations where every indicator screamed of deficit, disease, demons and desperation. Jesus acted as if provision was already done even when nobody saw it yet. The concept of balancing two realities underpins the faith way of living.

The expression, *Credo quia absurdum*, ascribed to early Christian writer and theologian Tertullian, translates as "I believe because it is absurd." This 2nd–3rd century saint faced the same challenge we do in understanding how it can "both be and not be" at the same time. He wasn't about to dismiss the apparent irrationality or paradoxical nature of faith. Tertullian recognized that belief frequently has to overcome human rationale and so he looked through what was "not" to what actually "was." Much appreciated, Tully. It helps to know that even you thought this whole now-but-not-yet thing is absurd in some ways. Thankfully, faith broadens our vision so we can "set (place) our affection (attention) on things above, not on the earth" (Colossians 3:2). Many times, that's what keeps us going.

THE BIBLICAL EXPRESSION OF SUPERPOSITION

All over Scripture we find mentions of this invisible REALITY present in another realm that surrounds our own. It's a world of spiritual possibility that undergirds and directs our physical world. The Bible again and again refers to this world beyond the five senses, a REALITY realized by faith and by spiritual perception. Consider these examples:

Faith as Evidence of the Unseen – "Now faith is the substance of things hoped for, the evidence of things not seen." (Hebrews 11:1). Faith acknowledges multiple possible outcomes and holds *evidence* for the unseen before it becomes tangible. Faith isn't blind belief but a confident assurance that it exists before it is seen. Faith sees not only "reality" but sees REALITY through a spiritual lens. Your miracle is waiting in superposition.

One of the great physicists of the 20th Century, Richard Feynman, illustrated superposition as "A phenomenon which is impossible to explain in any classical way, and which has in it the heart of quantum mechanics. In reality, it contains the only mystery." Feynman's choice of term as "mystery" resonates with me deeply because for centuries theologians have used this same word to define God and His works.

Jesus' Words of Completed REALITY

With the statement, "It is finished" (John 19:30), Jesus was speaking of an eternal, already-complete REALITY yet to fully reveal itself in time. He was speaking with a vision beyond the confines of the moment, accessing a realm where all the advantages of His completed work were already there.

"I am the Alpha and the Omega, the beginning and end" (Revelation 22:13). God has all possibilities in mind all at once, as if He sees everything in a quantum field of unlimited possibilities. Outside of linear time, He sees all points in time all simultaneously. Nothing about your life takes Him by surprise. God will never say, "Well, I didn't see this coming." You can be surprised by unexpected things, but He already knew and has prepared the response you require in advance.

The Kingdom of God Within

Jesus taught of this REALITY already existing but yet to be recognized (Luke 17:21). The Kingdom of God isn't somewhere in the far-off distance but a realty in reach of us. Don't look up or out and around. Look inward to the Answer and remember this verse: "All praise to God, the Father of our Lord Jesus Christ, who has blessed us with every spiritual blessing *in the heavenly realms because we are united with Christ*" (Ephesians 1:3, NLT, emphasis added). It's already been done. Now it's just about discovery.

Jesus and The Ability to Exist in Two Realms

Jesus operated in a way that suggests He was simultaneously fully aware of both supernatural and natural reality, like a quantum particle in superposition. He moved effortlessly between the temporal and the transcendent, demonstrating faith's power to rise above the physical world's limitations. You, just like Jesus, are a multidimensional being. The challenge is that your sensory perception can't perceive the eternal dimension. But, see it or not, you are there. (To be accurate, there is no "there." It's all actually "here," existing in different dimensions.) You are "in the world but not of the world." In other words, you live here but it's not home.

Walking Through Walls (John 20:19)

Jesus appeared in a locked room after his resurrection. This evidences the way He existed in both the material and immaterial realms simultaneously, moving between them at will. This occasion exemplifies what science calls "quantum tunneling." It happens when an object moves through another object. This defies our conventional understanding of physical laws and shows how Jesus was operating at a different level by functioning from reality and REALITY.

Multiplying the Bread and the Fish (Matthew 14:13-21)

Jesus entered into a REALITY in which provision was already full and brought it into the present realm. It was an expression of faith tapping into a source of abundance that lay beyond the restrictions of this physical world, illustrating faith's energy in actualizing divine provision.

What would it mean to see ourselves as equipped with this same ability? We can because we are! Jesus took five loaves and two fish, gave thanks, and multiplied them to feed over five thousand people. This miracle wasn't about creating something from nothing but instead accessing an already-existing REALITY of abundance. He didn't operate under the scarcity mindset of the material world. Instead, He tapped into the divine frequency of provision, showing that lack is an illusion when viewed through the lens of faith. He served lunch from a table they couldn't see but it was most definitely in their presence, in another kingdom.

Healing the Sick with a Word (Matthew 8:5-13)

Jesus spoke as if the healing was already done before it visibly occurred, collapsing the possibility into reality through faith. He operated from a perspective where wholeness was already real and healing was already available, and his words activated the divine power to bring it into manifestation. Others saw a sick person while He saw a healthy person. This can be frustrating to a sick person who doesn't see the objective REALITY but only sees their subjective reality.

Let's be careful to always be sensitive to those who struggle with chronic health issues. Some of my closest loved ones deal with ongoing physical challenges. We can't presume to know God's mind about the timing of the manifestation of anybody's wholeness. What we can know is that they are dearly loved by their Father and that He will always act in the best way at the best time. This paragraph could sound trite or even painful to those who suffer physically. The goal here isn't to minimize their struggle. That is the last thing I would want to do but I do want to lovingly recognize their situation and still encourage hope.

Jesus' ability to see beyond the visible symptoms was not a denial of reality but an awareness of the higher REALITY. It's the one where wellness already existed. The challenge for those who are sick or struggling is that they are deeply immersed in their subjective reality, their pain, their limitations, their circumstances. But faith is an invitation to step into God's reality, where healing, provision, and restoration are already established. The frustration comes when earthly perception contradicts divine truth, but Jesus' example shows that the key is not in fighting what we see but in shifting our focus toward what is unseen yet fully real. When we learn to speak from the REALITY of divine wholeness rather than from the limitations of human perception, we align with the miraculous flow that Jesus demonstrated. At that point, we either see the healing or know it is coming in God's perfect timing. Again, I am aware that to try to encourage faith while also trying not to sound calloused toward those who suffer is to walk a tightrope. I trust both the compassion and intended encouragement behind these words are sensed by the reader who is struggling.

The Transfiguration (Matthew 17:1-8)

At this moment, there was a change in Jesus' physical form as He was emanating light from God. It seems that His inner nature burst forth in an outer manifestation. This vision into his divine nature shows us what we too are as vessels of the divine nature we share with Christ. (See 2 Peter 1:4) You are a miracle carrier and possess the ability to manifest the Divine wherever you are. Let your light shine. Don't be fearful or shy about it. Just be yourself and others will catch sight of the Christ that lives in you. The Light that shines from you can light up dark situations where you find yourself and change them.

The Raising of Lazarus (John 11:43-44)

Jesus didn't see Lazarus as permanently dead but as existing in a state where resurrection was a viable option. His words materialized that REALITY into being. He recognized that death was not the final answer, and His faith allowed Him to access the power of resurrection life. Death doesn't get the last word. That's why we grieve not as others who are without hope (1 Thessalonians 4:13). I recall when my dad was nearing death in this world. One day, he told me, "I know this sounds absurd, but I feel your mother (who had died two years prior) with me often. When I am in bed at night, in the dark, she feels so real to me that I reach over to take her hand." My dad was already in hospice care and had very little time left to live. I replied to him, "Dad, sometime soon, you are going to reach over to grasp her hand, and she'll take your hand and walk across with you." A few short weeks later, when my sister discovered him dead in bed, his arm was stretched out to the opposite side of the bed—the side where my mother had always slept. He saw. He reached out. He went home. Death isn't anything more than a transition.

Each of these miracles reveals that a fixed reality didn't bind Jesus but instead exposed a state where multiple possibilities existed until one was chosen and manifested through faith. He demonstrated the potential for us all to transcend the physical world's limitations and operate from a perspective of divine potential.

OBSERVER EFFECT AND MANIFESTING MIRACLES

We have learned that observation causes potential to collapse into actuality. If we direct our awareness towards a specific possibility, we greatly increase the likelihood that it will materialize. Do you understand how faith works as the spiritual observer effect, monitoring what unseen reality becomes real? Quantum physics teaches us that we change reality by observing it, and faith works on the same principle. We choose a divine possibility, watch and wait for it to actualize. Your beliefs color your perception, and your perception paints reality."

The realm of the unseen is already full of potential. Our joyful privilege is to see with faith, bring divine truth into our reality by collapsing it, and walk in the miraculous as our natural birthright. The more we align our thoughts, emotions, and actions with God's REALITY, the more we manifest fully His Kingdom on earth. It's not simply a theoretical concept but a practical path to a purpose-filled, powerful, and divine-potential-filled life. As we take on the superposition of faith, we can start changing this world and manifesting heaven's reality on earth.

MIRACULOUS ENTANGLEMENT

You weren't designed by God to do life, or receive miracles, alone. Quantum science confirms what Jesus said all along: connection is everything. In quantum reality, entwined particles are still mysteriously connected, reacting instantly, regardless of how far apart they are. In the Kingdom of God, it's the same thing. You're not just close to Christ. You're one with Him. And you're inseparably linked with others as well, part of a spiritual network of love and destiny. Miracles don't flow independently to an isolated individual; they arise out of the union energy field— God with us, God in us, God between us, God as us. Christ lives His life in your unique expression of life. We are entwined for miracles, and that connection is the link for supernatural change.

Quantum entanglement is one of the strangest and most intriguing things in quantum physics. This instantaneous correlation, that even violates the speed of light, has puzzled and fascinated researchers for decades. It indicates that, in some mysterious way, they're not two but one. As physicist and philosopher Henry Stapp called quantum entanglement "the deepest and most important concept in the quantum theory." He's not alone in suggesting the primacy of this quantum phenomenon. It's noteworthy that quantum researchers, as a profession, argue that the greatest truth of science is the oneness present between all that exists. Union —that is the most important reality.

The last thing Jesus had to say before going to the cross focused on this topic. In His final prayer in John 17 (KJV), He prayed in verses 10-11:

> "And all mine are thine, and thine are
> mine; and I am glorified in them.
> And I am no more in the world, but
> these are in the world, and I am
> coming unto thee. Holy Father, keep
> through thine own name those
> whom thou hast given me, that they
> might be one, just as we are."

He then continued in verses 20-23:

> "Neither pray I for these alone, but for

> them as well who are to put their
> faith in me through their word; That
> all may be one; as thou art in me,
> and I in thee, so they too will be one
> in us: that the world may have belief
> that thou hast sent me. And the
> honour which thou gavest me, have I
> given unto them; that they may be
> one, even as we are one: I in them,
> and thou in me, that they may be
> perfected in one; and that the world
> may know that thou hast sent Me,
> and hast loved them, as thou hast
> loved me."

In His last words on the night before His crucifixion, He spoke of oneness four times. A dying man's last words always mean so much to the ones who are left. It's noteworthy that Jesus would say this not once but four times. We can only conclude that it must have mattered a great deal to Him. It would appear that grasping oneness must be incredibly significant. It makes good sense when you think that both Jesus and science affirm the priority in understanding this when we examine the nature of existence.

This scientific determination that entangled particles aren't actually different but are part of a system together as one, linked at a place outside space and time, disrupts the normal concept of locality and causality. It demands that we think outside the box. It reflects the truth that all things in all creation exist *in Christ*. Everything. Step outside of God, and you will find ... wait—there isn't a stepping outside of God. Theologian Paul Tillich called it when he said that God is the very "Ground of Being." Nothing exists outside of Him.

This union that goes beyond the confines of the physical world must be huge. Historically, wisdom traditions world-wide have taught that all things are interconnected. This isn't something new. At last, science is playing catch-up by discovering this same truth through contemporary findings. Scripture has always testified to a deep, abiding oneness between God, human beings, and the universe. It's thrilling to have science join the party!

Biblical Evidence of Spiritual Entanglement

The Bible shows evidence of a profound, interconnected reality in which people and God are mysteriously linked. The scriptures are filled with examples showing a REALITY where separation is an illusion and connection transcends the boundaries of space and time.

Consider how the Apostle Paul described it: "For we, though many, are one body in Christ, and each of us a member one of another." (Romans 12:5). There you have a biblical reference to quantum entanglement. What occurs in one part will affect the whole. Just as entangled particles are intertwined, so are we connected in Christ.

Just like one state of a quantum particle determines the other, we are defined by Christ. A quantum particle's identity isn't independent. Its state is determined by the one with which it's entangled. That's true of you too.

> "For you died, and your life is now hidden with Christ in God" (Colossians 3:3). You are not just close to God. You are *in* Him.

> "Christ in you, the hope of glory" (Colossians 1:27).

> "It is no longer I who live, but Christ lives in me" (Galatians 2:20).

We aren't independent beings trying to get close to Christ. It is not possible to become close with God because you already exist in a union with Him that's no less real than the linked-particle entanglement. Whatever holds true for Him holds true for you. Let that sink in—you are defined by Him.

Intercessory Prayer

"A righteous person's prayer is powerful and effective" (James 5:16, NIV). That verse isn't a metaphor. It's a quantum-level statement about how prayer works. When you pray for someone else, you're not lobbing words across a void, hoping God will take pity and respond. You're engaging the living network of divine entanglement. It's a place where their well-being and your own are already intertwined.

Prayer works like that. It's not a passive wish but an active energetic transfer within a spiritual system of oneness. When you pray for others, you're actually participating in your own transformation too, because we are all part of the same divine field in Christ. Intercession, then, isn't just requesting. It's resonance. You're tuning your own frequency to the frequency of the person you're praying for, and together, you both vibrate closer to the energy of God's love and wholeness.

This means prayer is more than a spiritual discipline; it's a spiritual technology founded in union. It bridges what looks like separation and reminds us that in Christ, we are all inseparably entangled. When you intercede for somebody, you are not standing outside their pain. You are standing within it, just as Christ does, releasing grace not only to them but through them and into you. It's all connected. Always has been. Always will be.

Binding and Loosing (Matthew 18:18-20)

Christ taught that whatsoever will be bound or loosed here on earth will be so in heaven as well. His words referenced a link between things done in one world and what they accomplish in another. It emphasizes the connection between the earthly and heavenly worlds and the reality that what we do here will have eternal implications in the afterlife. We have the opportunity to join together Eternal Reality and experiential existence in tangible ways.

Jesus and the Power of Relationship

Jesus lived with the full consciousness of divine entanglement. He fully embraced the reality that he never existed independently of the Father and that his disciples were forever united with him. This belief framed His ministry and empowered His relationships with others.

The Apostle Paul witnessed the same phenomenon in his own ministry and explained it: "To this end, I strenuously contend with all the energy Christ so powerfully works in me" (Colossians 1:29). He understood his union with Christ and how this energy operated through him.

Vine and Branches (John 15:4-5)

Our identification with Christ Jesus was illustrated as the branch attached to the vine. He is the true vine, and we have an unbreakable spiritual bond with Him. The branch and the vine symbol emphasizes the reality of abiding (acknowledging our union) in Christ and being aware of being linked with Him as the source of life and power.

The Power of Agreement (Matthew:18:19-20)

Jesus taught that a prayer request made by two agreeing together would be granted. Why? Because it is an expression of the principle of spiritual entanglement with His faith. This emphasizes the power of shared intention and the possibility of miracles manifesting when we are united in prayer. We don't get answers because we lobby God in great number.

What happens is that the "faith-force" for miracles is amplified when we are in one accord about a matter.

SCIENCE OF QUANTUM ENTANGLEMENT AND YOUR GRACE WALK

Considering the way entanglement causes entangled particles to communicate instantaneously, faster than the speed of light, we can better understand how prayer works. When you pray for others and circumstances that are outside your immediate space, your prayer takes on divine power. Your spiritual connection to Christ and your prayer request supersedes the confines of space and time and has instant effect.

By the way, Jesus is praying for you at this very moment. (Read Romans 8:34, Hebrews 7:25, 1 John 2:1, Hebrews 9:24) Consider the implications of that. Jesus Christ is physically in the presence of His Father, interceding for you. The one who's joined together *with* you is speaking with God *for* you right now! If prayer makes a difference when you pray for others, think of the implications of Jesus praying for you.

Entanglement goes against the laws of classical physics in the way it demonstrates union. It indicates that the universe isn't a collection of things that exist as isolated entities but as one unified and interlinked field inside Christ. All things are in Him. (See Colossians 1:16-17) Science is offering a spiritual truth that will change the lives of those who grasp and apply it.

We've talked about observation. Think about its power inside entanglement. What will occur when we comprehend this union and visualize our situation as being inside Divine Love? Can you envision it? Because observation influences outcome, when we are able to visualize God's all-pervading connection (not just presence) with all things in our lives, our belief will be triggered in a way that contains the potential for a level of transformation far greater than anything we've yet imagined.

If quantum physics tells us that observation influences reality, how much more could our spiritual vision shape the world around us? When we genuinely see, not just intellectually acknowledge but deeply understand, that we are entangled with God, we step into a REALITY where faith becomes the driving force in transforming our lives and world. When Jesus said, "According to your faith, let it be done to you," that statement pushes back on our wishing for things to change. It brings our awareness to the reality that we are empowered by Almighty God because of our union with Him. It aligns our temporal reality with God's REALITY in a way that brings manifestation to our lives.

EXPERIMENTS WITH INTENTION AND CONSCIOUSNESS

Research in consciousness studies has already shown that focused thought can shape physical situations. Can you see that this might explain how heartfelt, confident prayer exerts measurable effects on the subject of our prayer? We already have evidence that the prayers and intentions contained in the thoughts have a tangible effect on the physical world and that we can potentially shape events with the power of consciousness. Just think how faith in a benevolent God could energize that scientific truth.

If the physical world shows non-local connections, then the one where we understand our union with Christ must be working on steroids. It makes us realize how all creation shares a web of divine entanglement. I'm not saying that nature *is* God but that God reveals Himself *through* all His creation. It's a spiritual understanding that prompts us to rethink how we relate with the world and how all things are united inside God's Love. That awareness fast-tracks us toward miracles as a normal part of existence.

Living in Spiritual Entanglement

Learning about quantum entanglement can revolutionize the way we participate with our situation, relationships, issues, and every other aspect of life. This is how we can use this concept in everyday life:

Pray With Confidence

Believe that your prayers have an immediate effect outside of time and space. Anticipate results. Have faith in the power of your union with the Father, in the Son, and through the Spirit, and in the belief that your prayers are being heard and answered.

Develop Awareness of Oneness in Christ

Rest in Him each day by recognizing that you and the circumstances you experience are never divorced from His loving presence. Mindfully be aware of His involvement in each circumstance you face throughout the day. Sometimes a reminder as simple as, "God's got this" can be beneficial. Develop a conscious awareness of being united with Him in each moment.

Bolster Relationships with Others

Create unity among your relationships with people who are centered in grace, understanding that we are intertwined together in a spiritual way and that together we are stronger. Cultivate love, compassion, and supportive relationships.

Speak Life Over People and Circumstances

It's a demonstration of loving people when you don't just commiserate with them but stand with them in their hurt. There's a time to lovingly and quietly be present with people and a time to speak. Listen for the timing and urge them onward when the time is appropriate. Your well-timed words, spoken in faith, have the power to change reality for people. Use your words to bless, encourage, and inspire those around you.

Walk in Love and Forgiveness

Love vibrates at the highest frequency and reaffirms awareness of spiritual entanglement. Unforgiveness doesn't break our divine connection but it does interfere with our perception of it. Nothing will take away your union with God through Christ but some things will impact your consciousness and experience of it. There are ways you can optimize the space for miracles. Practice the virtue of forgiveness and create a heart full of compassion and understanding.

Have faith in the Power of Agreement

Unite your faith with others so that you can witness exponential effects in prayer. Join with people in concentrated purpose (faith) and elevated desire (prayer), with the knowledge that the collective power of your desires will magnify your request. If you doubt the truth of this, just try it.

Expect Miracles

By now you should be convinced that miracles aren't uncommon but rather the natural abundance that comes from a life synchronized with divine truth. While on the earth, Jesus continuously taught the power of expectation, instructing that faith would unlock the invisible into the visible. "As your faith be it unto you" (Matthew 9:29). Faith doesn't only hope for miracles; it expects them as a given, recognizing that God is already at work beneath the surface when the physical world shows no sign. Stop saying that God is *going to do it* and speak as if He is doing it at this very moment.

Faith is the spiritual observer effect that collapses divine possibilities into temporal manifestation. Expectation involves alignment and participation. When you expect miracles, you move your focus away from lack and into provision. ("My God shall supply all your need according to his riches in glory" Philippians 4:19). As you expect miracles, you rise above the limitations in your mind and become more aware of the unlimited possibilities by God. ("Is anything too hard for the Lord?" Jeremiah 32:27) You connect through divine resonance. The frequency of faith taps you into the supernatural current of the power of God.

To live in anticipation involves waking up each morning aware that the power of God is already at work, whether your senses are aware of it or not. The Red Sea didn't split until Moses raised his staff. Until the people marched in anticipation, the walls of Jericho didn't collapse.

Faith always comes before sight. Even when what you can see indicates the opposite, have faith that the invisible hand of God is making way for something greater than you could possibly ask and think. Have the expectation of miracles as a present reality rather than as possibilities down the road. The more your faith lines up with the love of God, the more you will be living in the supernatural as a lifestyle.

Practice Intentional Meditation

Aligning your thoughts and emotions with divine truth will strengthen spiritual coherence and cause your understanding of union to make your prayer more effective. Cultivate mindfulness and meditation to quiet your mind and connect with the still, small voice within. This practice is unfamiliar to many mainline Evangelicals, but try it and see the change it will bring to your prayer.

Act with Compassion and Service

As we serve others out of love, we cause divine reality to manifest. Let your actions be motivated by compassion and a heart for serving other people's interests, being aware that your actions will have a rippling effect. Quantum entanglement gives a physical explanation for the biblical truth that we are united with Christ. If we accept the truth of divine entanglement and acknowledge that we are one with Him, we enter a space where prayer isn't a plea but a power that changes reality. It's the space for grace to flow freely. The place where the power of love holds everything together in supernatural oneness and where miracles aren't stifled by human logic.

Living in consciousness of our oneness with each other and with God, we become a part of the quantum fabric of the universe. This divine entanglement holds all things in a state of perfection. It's an alignment that prepares us to access the miraculous potential of the very Life of God and become instruments of transformation in a world yearning for wholeness and healing. Once we accept the truth that we are one with Him and with each other, we can become agents in the response to the prayer, "Thy kingdom come, thy will be done on earth as it is in heaven."

CHAPTER 11

THE QUANTUM TRIGGER

Throughout our journey through quantum mechanics and supernatural miracles, we have observed how faith exists as both an observer and a facilitator. Faith collapses possibility into actuality and coordinates our lives with the current of God's power. Through entanglement, superposition, resonance, and coherence, each chapter has shown that what we previously described as "supernatural" actually exists as a more mature level of what is most natural of the Kingdom of God. Quantum phenomena show us how to move from doctrine to demonstration, where miracles are not only understood—they're undertaken in the unfolding of everyday life.

One of the central ideas in quantum physics is the idea of wave function collapse, the point at which infinite possibilities become one definite outcome. Prior to the collapse, quantum particles exist in the state of potential in a state of probabilities referred to as a "quantum wave." But the instant a person measures the system (observes it), the quantum wave collapses and one definite reality out of the infinite possibilities springs into being. This transition from one probability potential to one definite outcome is referred to by physicists as a wave collapsing into the shape of a particle. It's often called "popping a quiff."[1] It's one of the big puzzles of modern physics.

It is an inspiring gateway to the world of faith and the supernatural outcomes grace can produce. The Bible teaches that God's existence is one of unlimited possibility, an ocean with no bottom that has power to potentially cause anything you can imagine to become a physical reality. Faith is the bridge that collapses divine possibility into a specific physical thing. The reason Jesus spoke so often about faith as the determining element in miracles is because faith is the channel that moves outcomes from potential into the physical world.

Jesus instructed, "Whatsoever things ye desire, when ye pray, believe that ye receive them, and ye shall have them" (Mark 11:24), He was describing a process that involves a kind of quantum collapse. His words reveal the inherent ability we all possess to engage with and influence the universe. In 1 Corinthians 3:9 (KJV), Paul wrote, "For we are laborers together with God: ye are God's husbandry, ye are God's building." We are active partners in the work of God. This doesn't happen only by being observers but as active partners in His creativity. Your concentration embodies faith, and faith contains the power that motivates the action that leads to creativity.

QUANTUM COLLAPSE AND THE NATURE OF FAITH

Observation isn't a passive recording of preexisting data but an active participation in bringing outcomes into being. The saying, "Energy flows where attention goes" is on target. This is in line with the biblical teaching that faith is the "evidence of things not seen" (Hebrews 11:1). It's there but not yet seen. It reminds us that faith comes before physical realization. We don't need to beg God and then wait to see what will happen. Our faith can become a tool that brings out the solution to our prayers.

How Does Faith Cause Quantum Collapse?

INFINITE POSSIBILITIES IN UNSEEN REALITY

As the waves are in superposition and contain multiple potential effects until they're seen, so the unseen world of God's Kingdom has all potential outcomes before one is manifest in our world of time and space. The possibilities implied in this truth are staggering. Nothing is impossible unless we don't conceive it as a possibility. The unseen is filled with divine potential waiting to be accessed and molded by faith. All miracles, all breakthroughs, and all answered prayers exist in a state of potential before faith moves it to "collapse" it into our world. *Nothing* is impossible with God.

Look at how Jesus lived. He didn't talk as if possibilities were question marks. He acted and spoke with absolute confidence, knowing that divine REALITY already exists and needed only to be made manifest. In performing miracles, He didn't make the thing appear out of nothing but drew it forward from the invisible realm already present in the Kingdom of heaven. Faith isn't blind hope; it's the spiritual power that chooses and actualizes from the invisible realm of endless possibilities. Divine truth ends with an exclamation point, not a question mark.

As I discuss in my book *Quantum Faith*:

Faith doesn't cause something to come out of nowhere but causes it to come from Somewhere! When you see a dish on the menu in a restaurant and then order that dish, you expect that item to come to your table. Your attention is on it, and you are already imagining how much you will enjoy eating that meal; in time, it usually happens. (The quantum world is a world of probability, not absolute control.) When the meal comes to you, did you create it? Did it come from nowhere? No, it came from the kitchen and manifested at your table.[2]

Do you recognize the way faith functions within God's kingdom? Since all divine possibilities exist already, faith picks the one that actualizes in our world. When we align our consciousness with divine truth, we are co-creators with God within His creative power. This knowledge turns faith into an active force instead of a passive hope and enables us to approach the unseen world with the knowledge that what we believe calls into existence things that already exist in the world of potential realities. Faith doesn't wish; it works.

The world outside time and space has no bounds of finite constraints, poverty, or impossibility. It is the Kingdom of Kindness with abundant resources and God-given provision. Faith is the testimony that brought the unseen into the seen. When we choose to see beyond what's visible, we begin to behave as a human representation of Christ by moving in faith and not in doubt. It is then that we call into existence what already is and live in the miraculous as a way of life.

BECOMING A GRACE-FILLED WITNESS

Quantum physics teaches that observation turns a possibility into a reality. This kingdom principle has worked all along, even before it came to be known for what it is. Knowing the kind heart of God, we are empowered with faith to expect miracles that don't make sense. Consider a couple of examples of Old Testament heroes who were walking on this principle by faith:

The Battle of Jericho

Hebrews 11:30 in the KJV says, "By faith, the walls of Jericho did fall down after they had been compassed about seven days." Joshua and the Israelites circled the walls of Jericho seven days with the faith that the walls would come down. It wasn't their physical effort that led to the falling down of the walls. Their faith and obedience brought the unseen power into the world of manifestation. It didn't make human sense. The walls first didn't fall down and then people had faith in it; faith came before the vision and collapsed the word of God into tangible world. They first saw downed walls before the existence of downed walls. That's the way it is.

Elijah Calling for Rain

Elijah heard rain in 1 Kings 18 before the cloud showed up in the sky. His focus was beyond what could be felt or sensually experienced. He didn't panic but had a servant search seven times to find any hint of rain, recognizing that his faith would ultimately transform divine potential into a tangible result. He acted as if the rainstorm was already in process when a cloud showed up. His focus on God's truth, not on earthly conditions, defined what came next and the drought stopped. He knew he could always count on God and so he did.

Hannah's Prayer for a Son

She was barren; however, after praying to the Lord, she redirected her thoughts away from barrenness and toward giving birth. Even before she became pregnant, she changed her attitude as if the response had already been given. "Her countenance was no longer sad" says 1 Samuel 1:18 (NKJV). She spoke in faith by continuing to pray even when it didn't make sense, and then Samuel was conceived.

Gideon's Band of 300 Warriors

In Judges 7, The LORD spoke to Gideon and said to him, "You have too many men. I will deliver you with 300" (NKJV). God had cut down Gideon's army from 32,000 to 300 men. Despite the natural evidence that clearly pointed to defeat, Gideon had his mind set on what God had said and not on fear, and they emerged victors. Faith had created the possibility of a small, outnumbered army defeating an enormous enemy. And it happened just that way.

The Widow's Oil

In 2 Kings 4, Elisha encountered a widow who lacked enough oil even to feed herself. He instructed her to go get empty jars and to exercise faith that an abundance of oil would be provided to fulfill her lack. Things turned around the moment she kept her focus on the result of provision and not on poverty. The oil stopped multiplying only when the jars were all gone. Her jars ran out before her faith did. A focused affirmation triggered divine provision into her need.

Faith inhabits the world we experience

Can you imagine it? Joshua collapsed the walls of Jericho when he changed his mindset. Elijah felt rain even when there was no cloud in sight. Hannah changed the belief that she was barren and imagined herself to be blessed instead. Gideon imagined victory even when the odds were against him. The widow's oil multiplied in proportion to the possibilities of getting more.

What these examples teach are the capabilities of changing our perception in order to bring unseen realities into our world. Stop ordering God to do something. Stop begging Him and instead become the owner of the outcome you want. Faith is not passive; it determines what does happen in our world. It makes us responsible for what we think, what we say, and what we believe so we can understand how we create our world.

JESUS AND THE POWER OF FAITH

As we have repeatedly noted, the miracles of Jesus weren't random acts of divine intervention but manifestations of how faith reduces spiritual possibility into natural reality. When we see the quantum reality behind it, Kingdom laws start to make sense. Albert Einstein once said, "The most incomprehensible thing about the world is that it is comprehensible." He envisioned this order in the universe to be ordained by God. Miracles are not freaks of nature but truths when we grasp them through the quantum paradigm. It's another way of viewing things because it's the divine way of seeing things. It's God's way things were made to work.

My hope is to stimulate your faith to be convinced that you aren't passive when it comes to bringing possibilities to life in your circumstances. Having seen a few examples of Old Testament heroes demonstrate how faith brings the potential into the world, let's examine a few New Testament examples. Just remember, these New Testament heroes are not a different class. They were normal people like you.

Blind Bartimaeus (Mark 10:46-52)

Bartimaeus cried out in faith, refusing to accept blindness as final. Jesus responded to him, saying, "Your faith has healed you,' noting that the faith had triggered the miracle. Faith is not what generates grace. It's what connects you to it in a conscious, real sense. Bartimaeus's dogged determination to refuse to be defined by his blindness provided him with an open door to the miracle.

The Woman With the Bleeding Issue (Mark 5:25-34)

This woman's faith had brought her an understanding of God's power and made the potential of healing a tangible thing the very instant she touched the clothes of Jesus. Her urgency gave rise to an unshakeable faith and allowed her to tap into the power of healing that was emanating from Jesus. He told her that she had become whole because of her faith. Wasn't He the one who healed her? Of course, but her faith connected her to the outcome He offered and triggered the result.

These miracles show that faith doesn't respond to the way things are in the temporal but brings forth an entirely different reality from the transcendent world. Jesus existed with an awareness that there was always the divine potential, but it would be faith that would trigger it into temporality. His life was a dynamic display of the power of faith to transform the world.

It is Jesus who says that if your faith is the size of a mustard seed, you can say to the mountain, "Move from here to there" and it will be moved (Matthew 17:20). Faith turns an unseen possibility into seen proof. It reminds us of the power even of small faith to overcome what would otherwise be impossible things. It's not the size of your faith that matters. It's the Source and His faith has been given to you to utilize. Paul said, "the life that I now live in the flesh, I live by the faith *of* the Son of God." (Galatians 2:20, emphasis added) Don't pray for more faith. Just use the faith you already have. It's more than enough.

PRACTICAL STEPS TOWARDS COLLAPSING POSSIBILITY INTO REALITIES

If faith is a power that triggers the miraculous potential into manifested proof, then how do we cultivate it? How do we train ourselves to visualize the unseen so that we speak with authority and stay in an unshakeable faith?

First, we need to practice seeing transcendent truth beyond temporal conditions (2 Corinthians 4:18). Develop the vision to look beyond the physical world's constraints and see the superior reality of divine potential. Use your sanctified imagination to see through spiritual eyes.

Then, continuously think about the loving kindness of God so that His love becomes more real to you than earthly limitations. It is only when you are persuaded by His kindness that His promises are able to join to your consciousness and redefine your understanding of the situation.

Next, start a practice of noticing how God's work is showing up in your life and recognize that miracles are already present in your world. Exercise an attitude of gratitude for blessings already here, and know that more will soon manifest.

SPEAK AS IF IT IS ALREADY DONE

Speak faith-filled words about your life and align everything you say with divine potential and your Father's goodness. Speak words of truth that express your faith in God's promise and your belief in miraculous potential. Say it until you feel it. That's not faking it—it's *faithing* it.

Then, take action based on faith. Faith, alone, with no works to accompany it, is dead (James 2:26). Your actions give expression to your faith. Step into the situation just as Peter stepped into the water before it was bearing his weight. Step out into ways that align with your faith that God is on your side and has it already solved. Allow faith to lead your actions, even if they seem risky and irrational. Make bold faith steps in confidence that your action gives rise to possibility. Don't let fear cause you to freeze. Step outside of your comfort zone and take a risk in faith that God gives guidance and protection.

Be sure to watch against double-mindedness. James 1:6 warns that if one has doubt, faith will not be fruitful. Uphold unshakeable faith in the things God has promised. Create a faith atmosphere around you and remove negative thinking and fear. Seek out the relationships and the atmospheres that edify and encourage you.

Expect the manifestation you've prayed to see. As you grow in the skill of living in synch with His goodness, you will assume that miracles are the norm and not exceptions. Cultivate an open mind with the expectation that what is best will happen. Imagine that you're in an environment with grace surrounding you and seeing the goodness of God in every circumstance. If you don't see it on the surface, look down deep into it. "Imagination is everything. It is the preview of life's coming attractions," said Albert Einstein. Your Christ-ruled power of the mind has the capacity to create your world.

Jesus demonstrated that faith is the dynamic power to influence what divine potentiality becomes real. When He healed the sick, raised the dead, commanded the storms to be silent, and did all of the other miracles, He was demonstrating how to behave as we depend on Him and the power of His Father to create. Because we are Christ's people, we are commissioned to become a part of this same lifestyle. Conditioning the mind to sense what is hidden inside the Kingdom of God, speaking those words that express divine truth, and behaving in faith, we become allied with the mind of Christ. It isn't a passive role but an active cooperation with the Creative Force of the universe.

Faith is not some passive feeling or theological abstraction. It's the quantum trigger that collapses expected potential into experienced presence. Every miracle you've read about, prayed, or dared to envision already exists within the quantum field of God's goodness, ready for faith to call it into being. The world is not closed, predetermined, and mechanical. It is open, responding, personal. In this magnificent Kingdom, possibility calls out to the boundary of your awareness, waiting for your intention, your consent, your yes. What you see, believe, declare is what you will start to be. Miracles are not magic. They're mechanics: divine mechanics guided by grace, triggered by trust. The issue is no longer will it happen. The issue is will you collapse the wave?

CHAPTER 12

ACCESSING THE FIELD OF FAVOR

Throughout the course of this book, I have examined how quantum concepts like superposition, coherence, entanglement, and the observer effect all reflect spiritual realities that are revealed within the life of Jesus and the Kingdom that He proclaimed. We have learned that miracles arise from a law of love. A law of faith. And, above all, a law of union.

Each of the chapters has led us deeper into the workings of the miraculous, where faith is revealed not as blind faith, but as a force for creativity. A force working hand-in-hand with the God-designed order to actualize unseen realities into visible realities. We're not pleading with God for things He doesn't want to give. We're becoming able to see that He already did, and now we're getting involved with its manifestation.

And now we come to the source code of it all—the Field of Favor. This is the spiritual realm where it all starts, where all miracles have their origin, where God's mind conceives all things into existence. It is the world that Jesus inhabited, and the one that He said exists within you. I trust that you are moving beyond quantum mechanics theory and even beyond a miracle theology, and into the living, experiential reality of unity with God's mind. This is where doctrine becomes your destiny. This is where the consciousness of Christ becomes your center of creativity. This is where miracles become no longer surprising but instead are increasingly inevitable.

Spiritual teachings throughout history have all referred to the space of endless possibilities, a divine realm of infinite potential where all things are possible. Spiritual teachings in various cultures have spoken of this invisible realm as a place of unlimited creativity and accessible power. Learning, as we have in the past chapters, the kingdom of heaven can be more easily understood using the quantum concept. In that world, anything is possible to those who believe.

"We are suspended in infinite possibility," theorist and cosmologist Brian Greene said. It exists outside the bounds of time, space, and physical laws. What a great characterization of the kingdom of heaven Jesus taught is inside you! This vision challenges the orthodoxy many of us have been taught. Things aren't nearly so unchangeable as we've thought.

When the Bible references the mind of Christ (1 Corinthians 2:16) and the kingdom of God that exists within us (Luke

17:21), it indicates an inner human capacity for tuning into this divine Field of Favor we are always surrounded by, even when we are unaware. Because He lived with full consciousness of this reality, Jesus manifested miracles effortlessly. He illustrated how the awareness of this endless potential makes us co-creators with God in shaping reality according to His will. He invites us to transcend the paradigm of passively accepting what happens and become active co-creators with Him.

Carl Jung, the famous psychiatrist, highlighted the strength of the unconscious mind when he wrote that "until you make the unconscious conscious, it will direct your life, and you will call it fate." We must reject the common assumption that we will have to go through anything that comes our way. Instead, we need to access the unlimited possibilities that exist within ourselves. If the mind of Christ is the building block for life, we need to realize that we have more authority over shaping our lives than we might have known.

THE QUANTUM FIELD AND THE KINGDOM OF GOD

Sir James Jeans, the great physicist and cosmologist, offered a remarkable insight into the nature of reality that fits with both quantum theory and biblical truth. As science moved beyond the framework of Newtonian mechanics, Jeans was among the first to acknowledge that the deeper we look into the structure of the universe, the less it resembles a machine and the more it starts to look like something alive. He wrote,

"The universe begins to look more like a great thought than like a great machine."[1]

What a statement. For generations, the dominant worldview said that the cosmos was a cold, clockwork mechanism, something to be measured, calculated, and controlled. But with the rise of quantum mechanics, that paradigm began to erode. We discovered that matter isn't solid, fixed, or separate. At the most fundamental level, what we once thought of as particles are now understood as probabilities. They are waves of possibility waiting to be shaped by consciousness.

This led Jeans to suggest that mind, not matter, is the fundamental fabric of reality. That what we see around us may not be the result of random chaos, but the unfolding of conscious intelligence. In short, the universe may be less like a machine and more like a thought in the mind of God.

That idea opens a door to miracles. If the cosmos is mental at its core, if it is infused with meaning, intention, and awareness, then the world around you isn't passive. It's alive with divine energy, the life of God. The ancient Hebrews knew this intuitively. The psalmist wrote, "The heavens declare the glory of God," and Isaiah described how "the trees of the field clap their hands." Even Jesus said that if people kept silent, "the stones would cry out."

This isn't just a poetic metaphor. It's a spiritual truth and quantum physics is now suggesting the same thing. We live in a world charged with God's presence, but it requires a shift in perception to see it. This is where quantum and our faith come together.

To recognize the universe as a "great thought" is to realize that we really are living inside what some call "cosmic consciousness" and the Bible calls "in Christ." And we are not separated. We are fractals of that Thought. We are expressions of the Mind whose intention brought all things into being. The divine life is not something we reach toward. It is the Ocean we already swim in. It is God Himself. To quote the ancient mystic, Rumi: "We are a drop in the ocean and the ocean in a drop."

So, when we say miracles are possible, we're not calling out to some distant deity to break in. We're recognizing that the miraculous is already *built in.* Miracles are embedded in the blueprint of reality itself. And when we align with that awareness and tune our perception to what God has always known, we find that we aren't just observers of miracles. We are participants in them.

BIBLICAL TRUTHS HINT AT AN INFINITE FIELD OF FAVOR

God created the universe through quantum laws which exist as constants in the world. The invisible holds the building blocks of the world. What existed potentially in His mind became existence itself for us. It began in His mind and then became the material world.

Now pair that with the fact that we have the mind of Christ and think about the implications of that truth. The same Mind that created the universe into being, when the world first began, resides in you today. Has the mind of Christ weakened? Has His mind lost capacity because it's now inside you? Of course not! When you cooperate with His mind, the very idea of impossibility becomes almost ridiculous. Jesus taught that all things are possible for the one who believes. (Mark 9:23).

Faith is the spiritual muscle that moves the unseen realm into the physical world, acting as the catalyst that collapses possibilities into reality. William James, the man often referred to as the "Father of American psychology, explored the transformative power of faith, contending that by embracing certain beliefs even without prior evidence, we can experience personal transformation. James stated that "faith in a fact can help create the fact," suggesting that belief itself can bring about the desired reality.[2] In his work, *The Varieties of Religious Experience*, James noted that religious experiences often result in profound personal change, leading individuals to exhibit "the highest flights of charity, devotion, trust, patience, and bravery."[3] James' psychological viewpoint matches what the Bible teaches and quantum mechanics affirms. It's not magic, but it does often lead to miracles. God stands above it all, and the order of things is established in such a way that your thoughts will significantly impact the outcomes you experience.

THE ONGOING STRUGGLE

If you want to increase the likelihood of a miracle, stop looking outside and look inside your spirit. Miracles aren't events outside ourselves that we have to seek but potentialities hidden within us. Just as the quantum field isn't some distant place but a state of potential always with us, so too the Kingdom of God is inside you, waiting to be actualized.

Joe Dispenza wrote in his book *Breaking the Habit of Being Yourself:* "You are not wired a certain way for the remainder of your existence. You are consistently making your own world by the things you think, the way you feel, and the things you believe." It's the truth. You had the power to change your life all the time. It's time for Dorothy to wake up and realize the power to get home was always within her because, in a sense, she never left home. Stop trying so hard to "find" the power of God outside and start recognizing that the Spirit who resurrected Jesus Christ dwells in you and wants to work together with you in order to produce miraculous effects. You don't have to chase after miracles because you are already linked with them by being together with the Miracle Worker and His Kingdom. And the best part of it all is this—He's on your side.

JESUS' KNOWLEDGE OF UNLIMITED REALITY

Jesus is the model for what a human being is when we know our authentic identity. If you want to get an idea as to what you would look like if you were living at your potential, look at His example. He practiced and taught how physical limitations can be overcome by seeing ourselves inside the consciousness of God's very life. His example is a testament to the miracle that occurs when we believe the impossible and live from the mind of Christ.

He lives in you now, at this very moment, and invites you to operate from this higher state of awareness. This way of seeing changes us into active co-creators in our universe rather than passive victims of circumstance. Will you believe that?

THE ACCESSING OF DIVINE POTENTIAL

Jesus didn't live based on the restrictions of the natural world. He acted based on awareness of the greater truth rooted in His Father. How He lived His life indicates how He accessed the field of unlimited potential within the kingdom of God. We're talking about a Kingdom where physical laws are secondary to divine truth. It always puzzled people who witnessed His miracles, but it was normal for Him, just like it can become normal for us. Albert Einstein said, "The most beautiful thing we can experience is the mysterious," and to that, we all need to say, "Amen." Miracles are mysterious but not shut down by the physical world. They still ring out loud and clear for the people who have eyes and ears.

Look at these people who rose above the confines of the lower existence and found the indescribable joy of living with infinite possibilities:

Jabez—1 Chronicles 4:9-10

Jabez wouldn't allow his current conditions to dictate his future. Back then, the names parents gave children came with a reason. Jabez's own name had a negative connotation. It meant "sorrow" or "trouble." We have no idea what sorrow he might have endured, but what we do know is that he determined that his fate would not be defined by the limitations of his past, the conditions into which he had been born, but instead chose to envision a future greater than his current existence.

In the story of Jabez in 1 Chronicles 4:9-10, Jabez prayed, "Oh, that you would bless me and enlarge my territory! Let your hand be with me and keep me from harm so that I will be free from pain." His prayer appeared to confirm what his name had suggested that he had felt.

This was more than a repetitive prayer. You can almost hear the heightened desire (prayer) with concerted purpose (faith) and aimed at a Good God. That was a leap of faith that brought supernatural, eternal possibilities into a definite external result. He refused to accept his existence as one doomed to an unchangeable predestined fate. He saw beyond the liabilities of his past. He called out a future possible only with God. The one that existed in His unlimited provision but had not yet surfaced in his earthly experience. His prayer wasn't a passive, feeble wish. It was an activation, a knowing that the world in which he hoped existed already in the divine world, waiting to be summoned into being.

God's response came instantaneously: "And God granted his request" (1 Chronicles 4:10). His faith had caused a shift and put his destiny on a track of increase in all that he could never have conceived.

There was a quantum principle at work here. In an earlier chapter, we learned how quantum physics reveals the way a wave function collapses into a definite outcome when observed. Jabez's faith functioned as that observer effect, focusing on and fashioning a reality that had once been a possibility. His life demonstrates that unseen potential exists in abundance, but faith determines which version of reality we experience.

So, did God perform the miracle with Jabez, or did it happen by science? Yes! Real science is a tool in the hands of God. If a physician prescribes a medication for a sick individual and they recover, is it God that healed them, or the medication? Again, yes! Do you get the idea? For the umpteenth time, miracles are not magic, and we are doing ourselves a disservice by trying to confuse the way that God works with a "prayer-filled-pixie dust" that creates magic. God is teaching us today through science! Knowing His work is great, but learning His way is thrilling too, and a quantum understanding shows us that!

He made his ways known unto Moses, his deeds unto the children of Israel. Not His deeds, but His ways. In the book of Psalms, chapter 25, verse 4, the psalmist had prayed, "Show me your ways, Lord, teach me your paths." If that prayer reflects what you want, I am confident that the prayer is being granted even as you read. Like Jabez, your prospects aren't defined by your past.

Caleb—Numbers 13-14

Caleb stood at the crossroads between two worlds. One was defined by fear and limitation, the other by faith and divine potential. He arrived at the intersection when Moses sent twelve scouts into the Promised Land. Ten returned with a report colored by doubt. They saw the giants, the fortifications, and the daunting numbers against them. Their vision had been tinted by what had appeared impossible in the natural realm, and their conclusion had been the only possible one: "We cannot possess the land." But Caleb saw things another way. He gazed with Joshua into the same landscape, fortifications, and adversaries but through the promise of God. Others had seen a problem which made it look impossible, but Caleb had seen unlimited possibilities already provided. The land had already been promised. It had only been a matter of stepping in.

Numbers 14:24 records God's perspective on Caleb's faith: "But My servant Caleb because he has a different spirit and has followed Me fully, I will bring into the land which he entered, and his descendants shall take possession of it."

While the ten spies and the majority of Israel collapsed the reality of defeat into existence through their unbelief, Caleb refused to accept that version of the story. Their expectation was negative faith in action (fear), but Caleb saw (by faith) the infinite potential in God. Because of that, he stepped into the future that had always been available but required faith to manifest.

Defeat? That could have been the case. After all, they were outnumbered and all that the ten had reported was true. It was the temporal situation. However, there was a plane higher than that, a plane that was clearly a minority report.

As with quantum superposition, two possibilities simultaneously existed. Caleb's faith chose which reality became his lived experience. First, was the option in which he perished in the wilderness with the unfaithful generation. The other was the one in which Caleb entered the Land as a conqueror. His faith chose his way. He opted to see with the eyes of faith rather than human limitation, and that decision redefined his destiny. When you change your perspective, this same Kingdom law will work for you too.

Naaman—2 Kings 5:1-14

Naaman was a man of power, rank, and prestige. He was the commander-in-chief of the army of the Arameans, so he had become used to being treated with respect. Yet despite his stellar reputation, he had a disease that he couldn't overcome. He had leprosy. The disease branded him with the possibility of a future that could be drastically altered. When he heard that healing could be possible with the prophet Elisha, he traveled to him with wealth and prestige framing his expectation as to what his miracle would look like.

When Naaman reached the house of Elisha, he anticipated something dramatic. After all, he was a "big shot." Something special would be waiting for a person of his caliber. Maybe it would be a theatrical display of divine intervention followed by some great announcement by the prophet. Or perhaps a healing ritual befitting his rank. But instead of personally greeting him, Elisha dispatched a humble message: "Go and wash in the Jordan seven times, and your flesh will be restored." The message rubbed against Naaman's pride. The Jordan River paled alongside the great rivers of his native homeland. Clearly, if healing were going to happen, it would be done by a method fit for a general, not by such a mundane messenger and method.

His pride almost robbed him of his miracle. He walked away indignant, ready to abandon the journey entirely. Then his wise servants intervened. "If the prophet instructed you in a great deed, would you have done it? How much more, then, when the prophet instructs you, saying, 'Wash and be clean?'" (See 2 Kings 5:13). Their words struck a nerve with him. What if the miracle had never been in the water but in his willingness to give up his own agenda?

Naaman yielded. He humbled himself, walked into the water, and followed the word given to him. Seven times, he dipped himself underneath the water. When he surfaced the last time, his skin had been restored, as clean and smooth as a baby's backside. His healing had been present all the time, but he needed a change on the inside before a miracle could manifest on the outside. He nearly missed it because it didn't line up with his logic.

That's the way quantum reality operates. It won't be forced. We have to get in sync with what God reveals to us, not because He isn't willing for the miracles to happen in your life. Naaman's healing always existed as a divine possibility, waiting to collapse into reality by faith and surrender. His resistance almost kept him in the diseased timeline. It was when he synched with divine guidance that he entered another version of his story. It was one where healing already waited.

Which part of this quantum adventure challenges you the most? Will you be willing to accept the possibility that God can operate in your life in ways you have yet to envision? Does it all have to make perfect sense to you? Will it require giving up your agenda for how it has to happen? Every one of these events shows that divine power transcends natural limitations and logic. You aren't limited by things as they appear because, in the realm of the Kingdom of God, things are not as they appear!

Becoming conscious of the field of limitless potential isn't learning a religious technique or conjuring up supernatural encounters. It's becoming conscious of the REALITY that's always been. The Kingdom of God isn't some faraway location or some hope down the road; it's an immediate space woven into the very fabric of existence, waiting to be actualized with faith.

Quantum mechanics explains what spiritual seekers have long known - that unseen potential is molded by belief, perception, and purpose. Jesus lived His life in seamless union with His Father's heart. His call still stands open to us today: to understand as He did, to believe as He believed, and consciously cross over into the Field of Favor, where the fullness of divine potential resides. Faith is the bridge that makes heaven's reality a part of our lived experience. The question is no longer whether infinite potential is real because it is. The question is, will you *experientially* become one with it? Will you embrace the mind of Christ, where the possible and the impossible blend into the creative fullness of the Christ Life inside you? The invitation still exists. You have the opportunity to enter the field of divine favor and create alongside God.

CHAPTER 13

THE FINAL SHIFT: STEPPING INTO MIRACLES

As we reach the end of this path, one thing has become clear: faith and science aren't in contradiction but are intimately intertwined in a display of divine truth. Contemporary quantum physics and advanced scientific findings have started to open our eyes to what has long been stated in the Bible. We know that we are something more than most people know themselves to be. We know that reality is more malleable than we ever believed it to be, and that faith bridges the visible and what is not seen.

The miraculous is not a privilege of the extraordinary few but is the normal inheritance of those who live in line with the heart of God and embrace the mind of Christ. Jesus revealed a way of life that went against conventional boundaries and He challenges us to do the same. He talked about miraculous things. Not as metaphorical gestures but as real possibilities open to those who have faith. The question is clear: Will you assume the miraculous as your new normal? Will you grasp what God has shown through scripture and science and take a step into a life that functions outside of natural perception?

From Isaac Newton to Max Planck, from Albert Einstein through to the quantum theorists of today, there has always existed an underlying intuition that the universe is much more mysterious, infinitely more purposeful, and immeasurably more related to consciousness than we've known.

ENTERING INTO THIS MIRACULOUS LIFE

Understanding these facts is only the start. The challenge is in applying them. It's a matter of choosing to live the Christ life Jesus lived, to believe like He believed, and to demonstrate the supernatural as He did. The following are some fundamental takeaways we have discussed to engage the miraculous in your life:

Refocus Your World in the Context of Faith

Change from natural point of view to supernatural point of view and condition yourself to perceive problems as opportunities for a miracle. Trust that what can't be seen is greater than the things which can be seen (2 Corinthians 4:18).

Speak with Authority and Purpose

Affirm the truth in spite of circumstances because words

create realities (Proverbs 18:21). Speak life into your body, finances, relationships, and purpose.

Don't let doubt exist with faith but speak out of the certainty of God's promises.

Practice Coherence By Aligning Thoughts, Emotions, and Action with Divine Truth

Eliminate the inconsistencies between what you do and what you feel. Align your heart and mind with God's reality (Romans 12:2). Practice gratitude to develop coherence and spiritual openness.

Participate in Supernatural Expectation

Have faith that miracles will come to you on a day-to-day basis. Live with the idea that the supernatural is always present and can be triggered with faith. Reject religious skepticism and mental rationale that limits God's ability to move in your life.

Walk in Radical Love and Unity

Love is the highest vibrational frequency so live in it every day (1 John 4:16). Forgive quickly because unforgiveness disturbs spiritual flow and coherence. Serve and bless others, since the power of God flows best in unity (Psalm 133:1-3).

Act Boldly Because Faith Without Works Is Dead

Take faith steps even if the result isn't visible (James 2:17). Take on tasks that require a miracle with assurance, never limiting yourself to logic or fear. Don't let feelings cause you to stand down. Step up with courage and confidence, based on what you know, not on feelings at any given moment.

A Call to Step into the Divine Plan

Jesus lived as the ideal example of quantum life in faithful alignment with the Father with an awareness of the unseen world and in full involvement in manifesting the miraculous. He did miracles as a man who depended completely on His Father. He said, "Truly, truly, I say to you, the Son can do nothing of Himself, unless it is something He sees the Father doing; for whatever the Father does, these things the Son also does in the same way" (John 5:19, NASB). He later said, "The words I speak are not my own, but my Father who lives in me does His work through me" (John 14:10, NLT).

Don't make the mistake of thinking that Jesus was able to live a miraculous life because of His divinity. As His own words reveal, He did those miracles by the power of His Father who acted through Him in synch with the Spirit and the laws embedded in this world. You have access to *the same resources*.

The same power that brought Jesus back to life lives within us (Romans 8:11). The same power that quieted the storms, healed the sick, and increased resources is present today. But if you are to live this REALITY, you are going to have to renew your mind, accept the truth of who you are created to be and move ahead into the abundance of the Kingdom of God with confidence in Him.

What will you choose? Will you continue to exist under the bounds of human limitation, or will you tap into the expansive, supernatural world accessible through faith? Will you simply look up to God, pray and then wait to see what happens or will you live the Christ life inside your own circumstances and become part of the miraculous life He demonstrated?

The invitation is standing before you. Now is the time, not simply to believe in miracles, not simply to watch from a distance, but to live them. You were never created only to watch the miraculous, but to find yourself within it. The same Spirit that coursed through the veins of Christ now resides within you. The same quantum field of supernatural possibility encircles you. The same faith that created galaxies runs through your spiritual DNA. Step beyond the old realms of reason and restriction. Tune your heart to the vibration of God's love. Think with the mind of Christ. Live as though heaven is here, because it is. Miracles aren't magic, nor do they occur infrequently. They are the natural consequence of living within the will of God's goodness, governed by grace, animated by Christ's indwelling life. The veil is thin. The time is now. Enter boldly into the quantum life of miracles. It's the life you were created to know and enjoy.

Notes

1. Miracles Aren't Magic

1. C. S. Lewis, *The Lion, the Witch and the Wardrobe* (New York: Harper-Collins, 1950).
2. Albert Einstein, *The World As I See It* (New York: Philosophical Library, 1949).
3. Max Planck, *Das Wesen der Materie* ('The Nature of Matter'), lecture delivered in Florence, Italy, 1944.
4. Brian Greene, *The Elegant Universe* (New York: W. W. Norton & Company, 1999). See also Werner Heisenberg, *Physics and Philosophy* (New York: Harper & Row, 1958).

2. Miracles Should Be Normal

1. John Gribbin, *In Search of Schrödinger's Cat* (New York: Bantam Books, 1984).
2. Sean Carroll, *From Eternity to Here: The Quest for the Ultimate Theory of Time* (New York: Dutton, 2010).

3. Faith and Physics: Partners in the Miraculous

1. Benjamin Libet, *Mind Time: The Temporal Factor in Consciousness* (Cambridge: Harvard University Press, 2004). See also Dean Radin, *The Conscious Universe* (New York: HarperOne, 1997).
2. Herbert Benson, *The Relaxation Response* (New York: HarperTorch, 1975); See also Bruce Lipton, *The Biology of Belief* (Carlsbad, CA: Hay House, 2005).
3. Herbert Benson, *Timeless Healing: The Power and Biology of Belief* (New York: Scribner, 1996).
4. Dean Radin, *Entangled Minds: Extrasensory Experiences in a Quantum Reality* (New York: Paraview Pocket Books, 2006).
5. Meister Eckhart, *Selected Writings* (London: Penguin Classics, 1994).

6. Anton Zeilinger, *Dance of the Photons: From Einstein to Quantum Teleportation* (New York: Farrar, Straus and Giroux, 2010).

7. Andrew Newberg and Mark Robert Waldman, *How God Changes Your Brain* (New York: Ballantine Books, 2009).

8. Amit Goswami, *Science and Spirituality: A Quantum Integration* (Carlsbad, CA: Hay House, 2000).

4. The Mechanics of Miracles

1. Werner Heisenberg, *Physics and Philosophy: The Revolution in Modern Science* (New York: Harper & Row, 1958); See also John Archibald Wheeler, "Law Without Law," in *Quantum Theory and Measurement* (Princeton, NJ: Princeton University Press, 1983).

2. David Bohm, *Wholeness and the Implicate Order* (London: Routledge, 1980). See also John S. Bell, *Speakable and Unspeakable in Quantum Mechanics* (Cambridge: Cambridge University Press, 1987).

3. Beverly Rubik, "Energy Medicine and the New Paradigm in Health Care," *Journal of Alternative and Complementary Medicine*, 2002; See also James L. Oschman, *Energy Medicine: The Scientific Basis* (Amsterdam: Elsevier, 2015).

4. Amit Goswami, *The Self-Aware Universe: How Consciousness Creates the Material World* (New York: Tarcher/Putnam, 1995).

5. Richard J. Davidson and Antoine Lutz, "Buddha's Brain: Neuroplasticity and Meditation," *Scientific American*, 2006; See also Michael Winkelman, *Shamanism: A Biopsychosocial Paradigm of Consciousness and Healing* (Santa Barbara: Praeger, 2010).

6. W.S. Harris et al., "A Randomized, Controlled Trial of the Effects of Remote, Intercessory Prayer on Outcomes in Patients Admitted to the Coronary Care Unit," *Archives of Internal Medicine*, 1999; See also Larry Dossey, *Healing Words* (New York: HarperOne, 1993).

5. Prayer Is Action at a Distance

1. Nick Herbert, *Quantum Reality: Beyond the New Physics* (New York: Anchor Books, 1985).

2. Joe Dispenza, *Becoming Supernatural* (Carlsbad, CA: Hay House, 2017).

3. Albert Einstein, "Letter to Max Born," 1947. In Max Born, *The Born-Einstein Letters* (New York: Macmillan, 1971).

4. See Hebrews 11:3 (NIV) – 'By faith we understand that the universe was formed at God's command...'
5. Kerstin Uvnäs-Moberg, *The Oxytocin Factor* (Cambridge, MA: Da Capo Press, 2003).

6. FAITH SPEAKS AND REALITY LISTENS

1. John Archibald Wheeler, "Law Without Law," in *Quantum Theory and Measurement* (Princeton, NJ: Princeton University Press, 1983).
2. John Archibald Wheeler, quoted in Paul Davies, *The Ghost in the Atom* (Cambridge: Cambridge University Press, 1993).
3. Masaru Emoto, *The Hidden Messages in Water* (New York: Atria Books, 2004). While these experiments have been disputed by some, it is my view that the evidence supports the veracity of his findings. There are scientific fundamentalists who resist data just as there are religious fundamentalists who struggle with elements of theology many believe.

7. TUNED IN TO CHRIST CONSCIOUSNESS

1. Rollin McCraty, *The Coherent Heart* (Boulder Creek, CA: HeartMath Institute, 2006).
2. HeartMath Institute, https://www.heartmath.org/heart-coherence/science/
3. Mihaly Csikszentmihalyi, *Finding Flow: The Psychology of Engagement with Everyday Life* (New York: Basic Books, 1997), 2.
4. Mihaly Csikszentmihalyi, *Flow: The Psychology of Optimal Experience* (New York: Harper & Row, 1990), 71.
5. Ibid.
6. Ibid., 66.
7. Rollin McCraty, *The Coherent Heart: Heart–Brain Interactions, Psychophysiological Coherence, and the Emergence of System-Wide Order* (Boulder Creek, CA: HeartMath Institute, 2006).
8. B. Misra and E. C. G. Sudarshan, "The Zeno's Paradox in Quantum Theory," *Journal of Mathematical Physics,* 1977.

8. THE ENERGY FIELD OF MIRACLES

1. Masaru Emoto's water experiments: https://masaru-emoto.net/en/science-of-messages-from-water/

2. Watch the commercial: https://youtu.be/YG8K0yl4_hc?si=A6x59BMSZR b9Vch0

9. The Superposition of Faith

1. Brian Greene, *The Elegant Universe* (New York: W. W. Norton & Company, 1999).
2. Michio Kaku, *Hyperspace: A Scientific Odyssey Through Parallel Universes, Time Warps, and the 10th Dimension* (New York: Oxford University Press, 1994), 263.

11. The Quantum Trigger

1. This concept and the word "quiff" relates to the Quantum Wave Function.
2. Steve McVey, *Quantum Faith* (Lodi, CA: TWS Publishing, 2023).

12. Accessing the Field of Favor

1. James Jeans, *The Mysterious Universe* (Cambridge: Cambridge University Press, 1930).
2. William James, *The Will to Believe and Other Essays in Popular Philosophy* (New York: Longmans, Green, and Co., 1897).
3. William James, *The Varieties of Religious Experience: A Study in Human Nature* (New York: Longmans, Green, and Co., 1902).

BIBLIOGRAPHY

Benson, Herbert. *Timeless Healing: The Power and Biology of Belief.* Scribner, 1996.

Bohm, David. *Wholeness and the Implicate Order.* Routledge, 1980.

Born, Max. *The Born-Einstein Letters.* Macmillan, 1971.

Carroll, Sean. *From Eternity to Here: The Quest for the Ultimate Theory of Time.* Dutton, 2010.

Csikszentmihalyi, Mihaly. *Flow: The Psychology of Optimal Experience.* Harper & Row, 1990.

Davidson, Richard J., and Antoine Lutz. "Buddha's Brain: Neuroplasticity and Meditation." *Scientific American*, 2006.

Dispenza, Joe. *Becoming Supernatural.* Hay House, 2017.

Dossey, Larry. *Healing Words: The Power of Prayer and the Practice of Medicine.* HarperOne, 1993.

Einstein, Albert. *The World As I See It.* Philosophical Library, 1949.

Feynman, Richard P. *The Feynman Lectures on Physics.* Addison-Wesley, 1964.

Goswami, Amit. *The Self-Aware Universe: How Consciousness Creates the Material World.* Tarcher/Putnam, 1995.

Gould, Roy G. *Introduction to Electromagnetic Fields.* Prentice-Hall, 1962.

Greene, Brian. *The Elegant Universe.* W.W. Norton & Company, 1999.

Gribbin, John. *In Search of Schrödinger's Cat.* Bantam Books, 1984.

Herbert, Nick. *Quantum Reality: Beyond the New Physics.* Anchor Books, 1985.

Jeans, James. *The Mysterious Universe.* Macmillan, 1930.

Lipton, Bruce. *The Biology of Belief.* Hay House, 2005.

McCraty, Rollin. *The Science of the Heart.* HeartMath Institute, 2015.

McVey, Steve. *Quantum Life.* TWS Publishing, 2023.

McVey, Steve. *Quantum Faith.* TWS Publishing, 2023.

McVey, Steve. *Quantum Prayer.* TWS Publishing, 2023.

Misra, B., and E.C.G. Sudarshan. "The Zeno's Paradox in Quantum Theory." *Journal of Mathematical Physics*, 1977.

Newberg, Andrew, and Mark Robert Waldman. *How God Changes Your Brain.* Ballantine Books, 2009.

Oschman, James L. Energy Medicine: *The Scientific Basis.* Elsevier, 2015.

Pierce, John R. *The Science of Musical Sound.* Scientific American Books, 1983.

Planck, Max. *Das Wesen der Materie.* Lecture, Florence, 1944.

Radin, Dean. *Entangled Minds: Extrasensory Experiences in a Quantum Reality.* Paraview, 2006.

Rubik, Beverly. The Biofield Hypothesis: Its Biophysical Basis and Role in Medicine. *Journal of Alternative and Complementary Medicine,* 2002.

Teilhard de Chardin, Pierre. *The Phenomenon of Man.* Harper Perennial, 1975.

Wheeler, John Archibald. "Law Without Law." In *Quantum Theory and Measurement.* Princeton University Press, 1983.

Zeilinger, Anton. *Dance of the Photons: From Einstein to Quantum Teleportation.* Farrar, Straus and Giroux, 2010.

Zohar, Danah. *The Quantum Self: Human Nature and Consciousness Defined by the New Physics.* William Morrow, 1990.

Zukav, Gary. *The Dancing Wu Li Masters: An Overview of the New Physics.* William Morrow, 1979.

Endorsements

Twenty Grammy Award Winning Singer, Kirk Franklin said, "Steve McVey's books have been used by God to transform my Christian walk."

Dr. Tony Evans, President of The Urban Alternative wrote, "My good friend, Steve McVey, has put the amazing back into grace."

Gary Smalley, author of *The Language of Love*: "Few people have had the life change effect on my life that Steve McVey has had. Whenever I hear that he has a new book, I buy several copies."

Neil Anderson, author of *The Bondage Breaker*: "(Steve McVey's book) *A Divine Invitation* will enlarge your heart and increase your comprehension of God's love that goes beyond knowledge."

The late Bill Bright, Founder of Campus Crusade for Christ, wrote about *A Divine Invitation*: "Steve McVey has given us in very clear and understandable language a wonderful, indelible picture of just how beautiful, complete and even startling God's love for us really is."

Fourteen Grammy Award winner, Ron Block of Alison Krauss & Union Station: "Steve McVey is one of the voices unafraid to tell the whole truth about grace. Steve's biblical, solid, and life-changing writing points me to the freely-given love, favor, and grace of God in Christ—a grace walk experience.

About the Author

Best-selling author, Steve McVey is not here to sell you religion. He's here to flip the script on God —from cosmic scorekeeper to relentless Lover. He blends ancient Christian wisdom with quantum insight, mysticism with neuroscience, grace with grit, all to ignite a revolution of love. His  message? You were created to be loved, and to love in return. His mission? To help you see the face of God not in fear, but in friendship. Not as a judge, but as a joyful companion in your wild, sacred journey.

Steve and his wife, Melanie, live in the Tampa Bay area of Florida. They have four adult children and five grandchildren.

Steve McVey has written many books that address specific needs in the reader's life. His books are filled with biblical truth, practical application, humor and affirmation that will encourage and strengthen you in your own journey of faith. You can find all his books on Amazon. If you've been encouraged by *Quantum Miracles*, you may find his other books that come from a quantum perspective to be helpful too.

Quantum Life — Available on Amazon

Quantum Faith — Available on Amazon

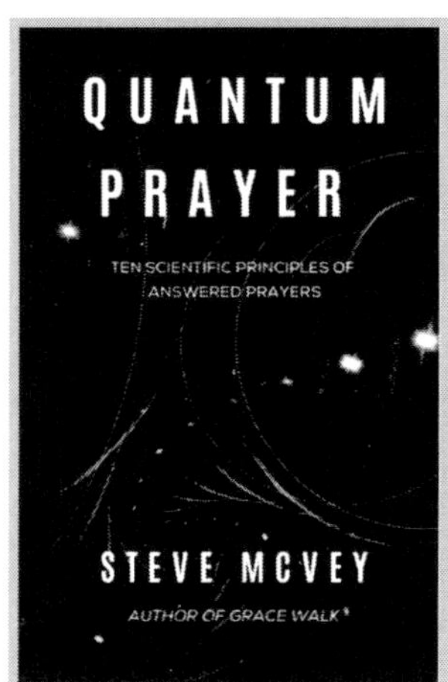

Quantum Prayer – Available on Amazon

Discover more from TWS Publishing—our authors, their books, and our growing collection of co-authored works rooted in grace and truth.

www.thewriterssocietypublishing.com

Manufactured by Amazon.ca
Acheson, AB